CIVIL WAR
CHARLOTTE

CIVIL WAR
CHARLOTTE

Last Capital of the Confederacy

MICHAEL C. HARDY

Charleston · London

THE
History
PRESS

Published by The History Press
Charleston, SC 29403
www.historypress.net

Copyright © 2012 by Michael C. Hardy
All rights reserved

Front cover, top: Refugees, from *Harper's Weekly*; *bottom:* Camp Exchange. *Courtesy of Harvard University. Back cover, top:* 1924 gathering of Confederate veterans and members of the United Daughters of the Confederacy, *Courtesy of Donna and Steve Poteet*; *bottom:* duel between the USS *Monitor* and CSS *Virginia* in 1862. *Courtesy of* Harper's Weekly.

First published 2012

Manufactured in the United States

ISBN 978.1.60949.480.3

Library of Congress CIP data applied for.

Contents

Introduction   7

1. Queen City or Hornet's Nest: Prewar Charlotte   9
2. "The War Commenced": 1861   15
3. "We Will Never Disgrace Our Native County":1862   27
4. "The War May Be Prolonged Indefinitely":1863   39
5. "Take Courage and Press On to Victory":1864   47
6. "Oh! When Will the Good Old Peaceful Times of '60 Return?":
   1865   55
7. Soldiers of the Gray and Blue: "He Could Not Die More Nobly
   or in a More Noble Cause"   69
8. Reconstruction : "We Are Tired of Turmoil and Disputes,
   and Want to Do All in Our Power to Promote Peace"   79
9. Remembrance : "This Will Be Our Last Parade"   93

Afterword: Looking for Civil War Charlotte Today   111
Notes   115
Index   125
About the Author   127

Introduction

In a 1919 journal article, James Walmsley attempted to determine the location of the final meeting of the Confederate cabinet. In contention for this distinction were Danville, Virginia; Abbeville, South Carolina; and Washington, Georgia; along with Charlotte, North Carolina. All of these places published postcards advertising a venue "where the last meeting of the Confederate cabinet was held." After exploring each of these sites in detail, determining who was present and defining what constituted a cabinet meeting, Walmsley concluded that "the last purely formal cabinet meeting of the Confederacy was held in Charlotte, North Carolina, April 26, 1865, in the upstairs west room of the residence of William Phifer." Despite claims by other locales, Charlotte was indeed the last capital of the Confederacy: it was the only place where the entire Confederate cabinet met after the fall of Richmond, Virginia; the papers of various departments were shipped to Charlotte and stored locally; the remnants of the Confederate treasury were deposited in Charlotte's United States Mint building for a time; and official acts, like examining and commissioning officers, took place there. After Jefferson Davis left Charlotte, the Confederacy effectively ceased to exist. Of course there is more to Charlotte's role in the Civil War than just the arrival of the Confederate government in the waning days of its existence. Charlotte contained vast and diverse government facilities and private enterprises that kept the Confederacy going.[1]

Seemingly countless scribes have written about the American Civil War, yet Charlotte rarely gets more than a sentence or two, and those are largely centered around Davis's arrival and subsequent flight. It is unclear why so many historians of the past have not found the Queen City important enough to devote scholarly treatment to her war years. It might be easy to assume that this is because Charlotte is largely a transient city, with people coming and going as times and industries change. Others might argue that there are simply too few primary sources. However, Charlotte was a thriving city in the 1860s, with three newspapers, three railroads and the beginnings of the city that it is today, leaving us much to examine in putting together the pieces of the puzzle to assemble a picture of this time period.

There are many possible ways to study a location. Historians could look purely at the experiences of civilians or of slaves. This volume focuses primarily on the military, the effects of the war on the civilian population, the roles the civilians played in government and military operations and the government and its facilities in Charlotte. Of course, the war was fought in such an all-encompassing manner that it affected everyone, from the oldest slave to the youngest child of a planter. They are all a part of this complex story.

Special thanks go to the librarians in the Carolina Room at the Charlotte Mecklenburg Library for considering my constant questions, many of which do not seem to have answers. Also, thanks to Julie Henry and the other librarians in the Special Collections at the J. Murrey Atkins Library at the University of North Carolina at Charlotte. Their help was fantastic. Once again, the staff at the North Carolina State Archives in Raleigh was a great help in tracking down pieces of Charlotte's past. Lastly, thanks to my readers: Jonny Alexander, Michael Ledford and Elizabeth Baird Hardy.

Chapter 1
Queen City or Hornet's Nest

Prewar Charlotte

First came the ancestors of the Catawba, following the *Eswa Taroa*, "the Great River," down from the mountains. For centuries, they lived, farmed and hunted along the river that later bore their name. European settlers arrived in the 1740s. Some of the Scots-Irish settlers—men like Thomas Polk, Thomas Spratt and Abraham Alexander, along with missionaries—founded a little village at the intersection of a couple trails used by the Catawba and the game they followed. A new county was carved out of Anson County in 1762 and was named Mecklenburg in honor of the homeland of the wife of King George III: Charlotte Sophia of Mecklenburg-Strelitz, Germany. The settlers at the crossroads complimented her even further, naming their village Charlotte Town. In 1768, a courthouse and prison were built, and the town was incorporated. The General Assembly declared Charlotte Town the official county seat of Mecklenburg in 1774. Hence the Queen City was born.

These early settlers were a freedom-loving people choosing to live on the frontier to avoid taxes and regulations imposed by the British government. In 1775, delegates from the different militia districts gathered in Charlotte. They passed what became known as the Mecklenburg Declaration of Independence on May 20, declaring themselves "free and independent." This was followed later that month by the Mecklenburg Resolves: "for the better preservation of good order, to form certain rules and regulations for the internal government of this county until laws be provided for us by the Congress."[2]

Mecklenburg County slaves picking cotton, circa 1860. *Charlotte-Mecklenburg Public Library.*

Numerous soldiers marched away from Mecklenburg to fight on the side of the Patriots during the American Revolution. The Revolution itself visited the streets of Charlotte in September 1780. British troops under Lord Cornwallis advanced from Camden, South Carolina, toward the Queen City, arriving on September 26 and skirmishing with the Patriots right in the center of the town. Cornwallis had overwhelming numbers, driving the Patriots toward Salisbury to the north. The British had control of Charlotte until October 12, when, following their loss at the battle of Kings Mountain to the west of Charlotte, they chose to retreat south. Cornwallis is said to have considered Charlotte a "Hornet's Nest" following attempts to mollify the local population. The hornet's nest was a name that stuck. The Revolution returned for a few days in December and then moved on to other parts of the South.

Charlotte remained just another backwoods town until the discovery of gold in the region. This early nineteenth-century discovery brought new businesses, immigrants and growth. By 1821, gold was being mined in streambeds in Mecklenburg County. Local farmers were soon exploring the hillsides and creeks, and local mines bore such names as the Queen of Sheba or the King Solomon's Mine. Others were simply named after the families who owned the property, like the McComb's Mine. In December 1837, a branch of the United States Mint opened in Charlotte. The mint struck gold coins in different denominations right up until the start of hostilities in 1861. With the mint in town, Charlotte experienced "an increase of trade and of employment for mechanics, new buildings were erected and all the vacant ones were filled…the circulation of money was more general."[3]

Real growth in Charlotte arrived in the 1850s with the appearance of the railroad. Talk began in the 1840s with an organizational meeting held in September 1847 for the election of directors. In 1852, the Charlotte and South Carolina Railroad reached the Queen City. Two years later, the North Carolina Railroad connected Charlotte with Goldsboro by way of Salisbury, Greensboro and Raleigh. Work began on another line in 1854: the Wilmington, Charlotte and Rutherford Railroad. The plan was to connect the port in Wilmington, North Carolina, with "the most direct route to the Mississippi Valley." While the line stretched west of Charlotte in 1860, the eastern portion had yet to connect to Wilmington.[4]

The population of Charlotte more than doubled between 1850 and 1860, from 1,065 in 1850 to 2,265 in 1860. Charlotte was the sixth-largest city in the state of North Carolina and boasted fifty-three merchants. Residents could purchase readymade clothing at Elias and Cohen's general merchandise store, groceries from William Elms, pharmaceuticals from E. Nye Hutchison or furniture from J.W. Sanders. A person in Charlotte could buy bricks from Taylor and Allison or flour ground in a steam mill by Leroy Springs. There was a furniture factory and a separate company that made sashes, doors and blinds. Possibly the biggest industry in the city belonged to Captain John Wilkes, who operated the Mecklenburg Iron Works. In 1854, a small number of the streets were macadamized. That same year, the telegraph further connected Charlotte to the rest of the world, or at least to the South. Residents of Charlotte could enjoy plays put on by the Thespian Club or visit the YMCA.[5]

There were two schools of higher learning: the Charlotte Female Institute opened in 1857, and in 1859, the North Carolina Military Institute started accepting young men.

Charlotte was also home to several newspapers, including the *Western Democrat, Charlotte Daily Bulletin*, the *North Carolina Presbyterian, North Carolina Whig* and the *Weekly Catawba Journal*.

In 1860, 36 percent of the population of Charlotte consisted of slaves, mostly belonging to members of the merchant and professional classes. Most who owned slaves only owned one or two. Thirteen of the slave owners were women. Only two of the men fell into the planter class: William Phifer owned

Constructed in 1858, the North Carolina Military Institute provided numerous officers to the Confederate army. *Public Library of Charlotte-Mecklenburg County.*

28 slaves, while James Osborne owned 23. Some slaves worked out of town on farms owned by their masters, while others were hired out as servants and laborers. The North Carolina Military Institute employed six males. In Charlotte, female slaves outnumbered male slaves 59 to 41 percent. Overall, there were 6,541 slaves in Mecklenburg County, with 290 free persons of color. The total population of Mecklenburg County was 17,374.

Like the rest of the white, male population in North Carolina, Charlotte and Mecklenburg County citizens went to the polls in November 1860 to cast a vote for the next president of the United States. On the ballet was Senator Stephen Douglas, nominated by the Northern branch of the Democratic Party. Vice President John C. Breckinridge was the Southern Democratic Party's nomination. The party had split in conventions in Charleston and Baltimore earlier that year. A third group, the Constitutional Union Party, whose platform was simply to support the Constitution and preserve the Union, nominated John Bell for the executive office. When the votes were tallied, Breckenridge had won the state, garnering 48,538 votes. Bell came in second, with 44,990 votes, while Douglas only managed to collect 2,701 of the votes cast. In Mecklenburg, 1,101 had cast votes for Breckenridge, 826 for Bell and only 135 for Douglas. Interestingly, Charlotte cast 372 votes for Bell, 195 for Breckenridge and 76 for Douglas. The eventual winner of the presidential election, Abraham Lincoln, failed to muster enough support to even get on the ballot in North Carolina, gaining no votes. The newly formed Republican Party advocated business, high tariffs, internal improvements and social reforms. There were many in the Deep South who believed that the election of a Radical Republican to the presidency would be the death blow to the United States. Not long after the confirmation of Lincoln's election, the Deep South states began to leave the Union.[6]

All of the hopes and dreams of the many citizens of the Queen City were shattered by news coming across the telegraph lines from Charleston, South Carolina, on December 19, 1860: "The Union is dissolved."

Chapter 2

"The War Commenced"

1861

W e noticed," declared the *Charlotte Daily Bulletin* on December 1, 1860, "yesterday morning, floating from the cupola on the large Brick Building on Trade Street…a plain Blue Flag with a White Star in the centre—a 'Lone Star,' hoisted, no doubt, by a true resistance man." While many in North Carolina followed the lead of Raleigh newspaper editor William Holden, adopting a "watch and wait" attitude, not many Charlotte residents embraced that strategy. The *Charlotte Daily Bulletin* article went on to state that cockades were beginning to appear and that Mecklenburg citizens were as "anxious to throw off the yoke put upon her sons by yankee abolitionists" as their ancestors had been to proclaim their independence from King George III in 1775.

As 1860 drew to an end, meetings regarding the present state of affairs were beginning to take place all across North Carolina. The first meeting advocating secession was held in Cleveland County on November 12, 1860. Pro-Union meetings soon followed. Sometimes, it was hard to differentiate between the two. The Charlotte newspapers called for a gathering "without distinction of party" at the Mecklenburg County Courthouse at noon on Saturday, December 1. Newspaper editor William Yates called on local citizens to remember "those incorruptible patriots who knew their rights and dared maintain them at any cost" and asked if his fellow citizens were "willing to submit to…injustice and unmitigated degradation." For Yates, that injustice had spanned at least thirty years, in which "the people of the South [have] been oppressed and insulted, their Institutions assailed, and their rights invaded, and they have borne oppression with meekness until the cup of their degradation has been filled by the election of a man to the Presidency who stands pledged to overthrow their Institutions."[7]

On the appointed day, a crowd gathered at the courthouse. James Robinson was appointed chairman, with John Brown and M.L. Wallace designated secretaries. A committee of eleven, with John A. Young as chairman, was appointed to draft a resolution, and while they met, "brief but pertinent speeches" were given to assembled masses by William Myers, Daniel Hill, Charles Lee and John Brown, among others. It took more than two hours for Young to report back with the resolutions drafted by the committee. The resolution stated that the election of Lincoln and his vice president, Hannibal Hamlin, had been brought about by a "sectional organization, predicated upon a sentiment embodying the doctrine of the 'irrepressible conflict,'" and "that a house divided against itself cannot stand." The committee believed that this course was "subversive of the purposes our fathers had in view in the formation of our Federal Government." Not only were the perceived designs of Lincoln and the other Republicans unconstitutional, but they sought to make war against "our domestic tranquility, peace and happiness, by stimulating our slaves to insubordination, insurrection and rebellion and thereby imperiling our lives and those of our wives and our children." For many Charlotte residents, the failed insurrection of abolitionist John Brown was more than just words on a page: Pikes manufactured for Brown, to be given to those who joined his band at the Federal Arsenal at Harpers Ferry, were housed in the North Carolina Military Institute.[8]

"Be it therefore Resolved," continued the committee, that the "sentiment which has produced the crisis" is engulfing the country. The committee believed that the Legislature then meeting in Raleigh should prepare to act, to call a convention for the purpose "of going into calm, considerate and dignified counsel for the preservation of our Union and our Federal government." If that did not work, then steps should be taken to protect the rights of the people of North Carolina. If other states were to withdraw from the Union, North Carolina should be ready to pursue "a similar course of action." The resolutions were then passed "without a dissenting voice" and sent to the local papers for publication and to the Mecklenburg representatives in the General Assembly.[9]

A pro-Union meeting was held at Wallis's Steam Mill on December 21. Many of the same people were present at both meetings. John Young, who drafted the resolutions at the secession meeting, delivered a "very eloquent and patriotic address." R.L. DeArmon was called on to chair the meeting, and Joseph Gillespie led the committee that drafted the resolutions. The committee, in these resolutions, "sadly deplored" the election of Lincoln, "a sectional man." Yet they believed that his election was legitimate, and as loyal citizens, "we should acquiesce, so long as he remains a *constitutional* president." Should the president overstep his constitutional bounds, and if the courts were unable to restrain Lincoln, then Mecklenburg citizens "should invoke the spirit of our revolutionary fathers to fire our hearts and nerve our arms for the revolution without delay." At the same time, attendees called for a convention "in order that she may be prepared to assert her position and her rights in any emergency." Mecklenburg seemed to be

James Dinkins was a cadet at the North Carolina Military Institute when the war began. He later fought under Confederate cavalry leader Nathan Bedford Forrest. *From* 1861 to 1865 by an Old Johnnie *(1897).*

split into two camps: those advocating immediate secession, and those wishing to wait until Lincoln clearly overstepped his constitutional bounds. While such meetings espoused one side of the issue or the other, more often the secession platform became common. There was a meeting at Morrow's Turn Out (present-day Pineville) in mid-December. Two public meetings were held on February 5, one at the courthouse and another at Barryhill's School House.[10]

However, North Carolina was not ready to pursue any action beyond words and resolutions. South Carolina, Mississippi, Florida, Alabama, Georgia, Louisiana and Texas all passed ordinances of secession by February 1, 1861. Three days later, delegates from these states met and organized the Confederate States of America, with former Secretary of War and Mississippi senator Jefferson Davis as provisional president.

North Carolina governor John Ellis, in his message to the General Assembly in December 1860, believed that Lincoln's election endangered the rights of the states and that a convention of North Carolinians should be called to consider the question of withdrawing the state from the Union. On January 24, 1861, an act was passed calling for a vote on whether to call a convention and to elect delegates based on a county's representation in the House of Commons. Four candidates emerged in Mecklenburg County. The secessionist candidates, as elected by delegates from the different "heats" on February 7, were William Johnston, president of the Charlotte and South Carolina Railroad, and James Osborne, a state judge. Joseph H. Wilson and Robert Davidson were the other delegates. Before the vote was actually taken, Wilson and Davidson withdrew, believing that "there is really no difference between the candidates" and that in this time "of great importance that we should all be united in the present crisis." Men gathered at polls across the state on February 28, casting 47,322 votes against calling the convention, with 46,672 for the convention. Just 650 votes kept North Carolina in the Union. The vote in Mecklenburg County was nowhere near those margins: 1,448 for the convention, 252 against. In Charlotte, 747 men voted for the convention, while 7 were opposed. Johnston and Osborne won by landslides.[11]

The failure of a Peace Conference in Washington, D.C., coupled with Lincoln's inaugural address, drove many into the Secessionist ranks. Another factor was the rise of the Southern Rights Party. A joint meeting, with people from Mecklenburg, Gaston, Rowan and Cabarrus Counties, was held in Charlotte on March 16, 1861. Dr. J.F. Gilmer of Cabarrus was elected president. The Honorable Burton Craig and Victor Barringer spoke to the masses while a committee drafted resolutions. Despite 93,994 votes cast, these men believed that "a fair expression of the public will has not been obtained." So they advocated electing delegates to a state-wide meeting in Goldsboro on March 22–23. Once the joint meeting was over, the Mecklenburg County citizens went into session and elected fifty delegates to attend that meeting. It seemed that mass public meetings were held at least every weekend. There was one in the courthouse on April 22, advising the justices of the county to appropriate the amounts they thought proper to support the volunteer companies being formed.[12]

On April 16, the *Western Democrat* declared "THE WAR COMMENCED." According to the article, local citizens had raised $130 to pay the telegraph company for the latest news coming out of Charleston. "This result," continued the paper, "will make every true southern heart rejoice." When

James H. Lane was a professor at the North Carolina Military Institute at the start of the war. He went on to command a brigade in the Army of Northern Virginia. *Auburn University.*

the news made it to the streets of Charlotte, William Myers and John Young were called out and made speeches to the public. Included in the evening's affairs was a salute fired in honor of the Confederate victory at Fort Sumter in Charleston.[13]

War fever gripped the Queen City. The cadets at the North Carolina Military Institute went to Professor James H. Lane, asking him if he objected "to their raising a Confederate flag on the building early the next morning and firing an artillery salute as the train passed by." Lane simply told the cadets that they knew of his habits and that he "did not expect to change my hour of rising." The "Next morning, long before sunrise, there was a 'secesh flag' floating from the barracks, made and presented by the patriotic ladies of the town; and when the train passed on its way to South Carolina the artillery thundered forth its greetings…Every window on the train was open with eager heads thrust out, the men yelling and waving their hats…The engineer made his whistle scream as it had never screamed before," recalled a professor from the school.[14]

Lincoln issued a proclamation on April 15 declaring that an insurrection existed and sent out a call for seventy-five thousand troops to go into the South and crush the rebellion. The Charlotte papers published Lincoln's call, along with Governor Ellis's response: "I can be no party to this violation of the laws of the country and to this war upon liberties of a free people. You can get no troops from North Carolina." Ellis moved quickly, ordering the forts along the coast seized, along with the arsenal in Fayetteville. On April 20, the United States Mint in Charlotte fell to a local company, the Charlotte Grays. Ellis later offered the mint to Jefferson Davis, to produce coins for the Confederacy. The same day the mint was captured, Ellis ordered the state legislatures into special session. On May 1, the General Assembly passed a bill calling for the May 13 election of 120 delegates. These delegates met in Raleigh on May 20.[15]

Not everyone was a committed secessionist, despite the rhetoric in the newspapers. John Morehead stated in 1865 that "he had always been opposed to the doctrine of secession." James Morrow proclaimed himself a Union man. John Blackwood, president of the Charlotte Bank, stated after the war that he had voted for Bell in the presidential election, "hoping his election might prevent if possible the threatened disruption of the Union. When a Convention was first called for in the state, I voted in the negative, but after the State of Virginia Seceded and hostilities actually commenced, another Convention was called for, and in that instance, voted for the convention." There were probably a few more like Morehead and Burrow, staunch Unionists,

The United States Mint in Charlotte was captured by local militia in 1861. *Public Library of Charlotte-Mecklenburg County.*

and probably many more like Blackwood, conditional Unionists who changed their minds once Virginia left the Union, and the cannons fired at Fort Sumter. We will probably never know how many fell into each category.[16]

William Johnston and James Osborne were again the delegates from Mecklenburg. One historian once considered the group that met in Raleigh "one of the ablest political bodies ever assembled in North Carolina." At 5:30 that afternoon, a man stepped out onto the west balcony of the state capitol and signaled to those below: North Carolina had adopted an ordinance of secession. Delegates signed the ordinance the following day. It was a momentous day, coinciding with the eighty-sixth anniversary of the Mecklenburg Declaration of Independence.[17]

Men from Mecklenburg had not waited for the state to act before enlisting. A militia system had existed for decades prior to the war. Each county in the state fielded a militia regiment. Mecklenburg County contained two: the Eighty-fifth and the Eighty-sixth Regiment. The county was then divided up into different militia districts, with a captain in charge of each district.

Each regiment was required to drill annually. Unfortunately, in many ways, the militia was ineffectual, and the annual gatherings were often social engagements. In 1858, the Hornet's Nest Riflemen were organized as a private militia group. William Lewis was captain. Private militia groups were common in large cities both North and South. They often had custom uniforms and privately purchased weapons. Drills and public parades were held frequently. A second private militia company was organized January 26, 1861: the Charlotte Grays. Egbert Ross was elected captain. While Ross was just nineteen years old, he was also a cadet at the Hillsborough Military Academy. Most of the Charlotte Grays were between eighteen and twenty-two years old. A third company was formed in early April, proudly naming themselves the Ranaleburg Riflemen. Albert Erwin was elected captain.[18]

A typical infantry company of the time period was composed of one hundred men. The captain commanded the company, aided by two or three lieutenants. These positions were elected. The noncommissioned officers, sergeants and corporals, were usually appointed by the captain. Finally came the privates in the ranks. Forming new companies was usually done via word of mouth or, in large cities like Charlotte, through the local newspaper. The May 28, 1861 edition of the *Western Democrat* found advertisements from Thomas Brem, who was recruiting for an artillery battery; James Miller, who was forming a cavalry company; and W. Lee Davidson, who was recruiting for an infantry company. Each advertisement offered new recruits fifteen dollars in bounty money, plus the promise of uniforms, arms and medical care. Once the required number of men had been reached, the captain usually tendered the services of the regiment to the governor. Not all regiments were accepted. In late April 1861, J.B. Robinson from Pineville tendered his cavalry company to the state. Adjutant General John Hoke wrote Robinson on April 27, advising that there was "no need of mounted troops" yet. It would be better if Robinson worked on forming an infantry company. Cavalrymen were expected to provide their own mounts.[19]

Governor Ellis ordered the Hornet's Nest Riflemen to Fort Caswell in late April. Before they set off, a group of Charlotte ladies presented the company with a flag. Miss Laura Sadler delivered the address, reminding the soldiers of their Revolutionary forebears, charging them with the protection of the flag. "Vigilant in preparing for difficulties," Sadler concluded, "firm in resisting oppression, and brave in defending our rights—the Hornet's Nest Riflemen stand prepared for every emergency." The presentation of a flag by the ladies of Charlotte would be repeated often over the next year.[20]

Soon thereafter, Major Daniel Hill received orders to transfer the bulk of the cadets at the North Carolina Military Institute to Raleigh, to serve as drill masters for the numerous companies arriving at various camps of instruction in the area. Governor Ellis soon ordered the formation of the First North Carolina Volunteers. Hill was promoted to colonel of the regiment, while two other professors from the institute, Charles Lee and James Lane, were promoted to lieutenant colonel and major. Two of the Mecklenburg companies, the Hornet's Nest Riflemen and the Charlotte Grays, were incorporated into the regiment. Most regiments of the time were composed of ten companies of one hundred men each. After the first days of the war, however, companies and regiments were seldom at full strength. It was while the regiment was in Raleigh that the first of many wartime deaths occurred. James Hudson, a member of the Hornet's Nest Rifleman, died of pneumonia on May 11. Hudson's remains were sent to the railroad depot, where his company fired a salute in his honor before the train left for Charlotte.[21]

The men of the First North Carolina Volunteers were transferred to Virginia and stationed on the peninsula below Richmond. On June 10, Hill's regiment engaged the Federals at Big Bethel Church, a resounding Confederate victory. The Federals were forced to retreat, and the Charlotte newspapers sang the praises of the Tar Heels. A rifle and knife captured from the Federal troops were sent back to Charlotte where John Springs displayed them for decades after the war.[22]

There were more Charlotte and Mecklenburg County men joining Confederate service. Robert McKinney, another professor at the North Carolina Military Institute, recruited an infantry company that became Company A, Sixth North Carolina State Troops on May 16, 1861. Merchant William Davidson also recruited a company, which became Company D, Seventh North Carolina State Troops on May 16. The Ranaleburg Riflemen chose to elect Albert Erwin as captain. They became Company B, Thirteenth North Carolina Troops also in May 1861. Another merchant, Thomas Brem, recruited the "Charlotte Artillery." Several of Brem's recruits were Irish. Brem was considered "one of the most patriotic men in the state." He "advanced the money to fully equip the battery, besides informing and feeding the men and purchasing eighty head of horses." The Charlotte Artillery became Company C, First North Carolina Artillery, on August 15, 1861. Many of these companies, while still in Mecklenburg County, were treated to lavish banquets. One such "public dinner" was held at Mallard Creek Church for the benefit of the "Mecklenburg Farmers," a company being organized by John Alexander.

After a morning of drill, the recruits were marched to the tables "and partook of an excellent dinner." The men and their host afterward proceeded to the speaker's stand, where three different ministers gave "beautiful and well conceived speeches abounding in practical common sense and good advice." Often, this scene was repeated as the soldiers prepared to leave: a public dinner, followed by prayer and a speech to the soldiers off on their journey.[23]

The "town is really deserted, day after day adds to the absentees," wrote John Wilkes to his wife in August 1861. "The male population is really decimated." By the first of 1862, Mecklenburg County had sent 921 men to the Confederate army. The

Brothers Henry and Levi Walker both joined Company B, Thirteenth North Carolina State Troops on May 20, 1861. Each lost a leg during the Gettysburg campaign. *North Carolina Museum of History.*

start of hostilities produced many changes to the town itself. Some businesses closed; others opened. The *Charlotte Daily Bulletin* went from four pages to two. The *Western Democrat* asked forgiveness for the quality of its ink, not being able to get any through the blockade, and claimed, "Now is the time to patronize southern enterprise." Gone were the advertisements for *The Congressional Globe* and Northern resorts. Anne Atkins McAllister, a student at the Charlotte Female Institute, left with other students and returned to Fayetteville at the start of the war. Even with some of the students leaving, the school remained open throughout the war.[24]

Many new wartime-related businesses sprang up in Charlotte. Both the tailoring firms of J. Smith Phillips and Fullings & Springs had contracts to manufacture clothing for the army and had called on the services of "scores of the daughters of Mecklenburg County" to help produce the uniforms. Pritchard and Shaw, along with S.M. Howell, were making "saddles, bridles, harness, belting, strapping, cartridge boxes, &c.," for the army. J.H. Stevens and Company established a firm in the fall of 1861 to manufacture envelopes. The business was directly opposite the post office. The Rock Island Woolen Mill, on Tuckaseegee Road, began manufacturing jackets for the Confederate army.[25]

Possibly the busiest place in town became the combined passenger and separate freight depots for the Charlotte and South Carolina Railroad and the North Carolina Railroad. These two lines were of two different gauges. Throughout most of the war, this created a logistical nightmare. Added to this was a shortage of cars, both for freight and passengers. There were no facilities to keep waiting engines and cars out of the weather, and passengers often had to wade through the mud to various points. At one point, a South Carolina railroad refused to allow its cars to be taken to Charlotte, to sit on sidings to be used as "emergency warehouses."[26]

In contrast, many citizens of Charlotte were less resistant to lending a hand in the early days of the conflict. When the Hornet's Nest Rifles boarded the train to head off to war, "every article worn, with the sole exception of their shoes, were evolved by the busy fingers of Charlotte ladies. This labor extended even to the production of caps. A pattern for the caps was obtained by…John Springs and the first cap was made by his wife…Elizabeth C. Springs…The pattern was later copied in many homes, where the uniforms were being made, socks knitted, and underwear made." Other groups made contributions of various kinds. In late June 1861, the "Jewish ladies" of Charlotte gave the mayor $150 "for the benefit of the families of volunteers who have gone off to the war." Charlotte had a sizable Jewish population, many of whom, such as the diarist Louis Leon, enlisted in the Confederate army. "Let all who can, imitate the example of the 'Jewish ladies,' and give something to clothe and feed the poor" admonished the *Western Democrat.*[27]

Contributions by the ladies of Charlotte went beyond making clothing and raising money. In July 1861, the Ladies Hospital Association of Mecklenburg County was formed. Its purpose was to "alleviate the suffering of our brave soldiers at Yorktown." Within a few days of organization, the ladies had already raised five hundred dollars and sent nurses to Virginia. "Mrs. Bolton, Miss Catherine Gibbon, and a colored woman named Nancy…were furnished with supplies and sent to Yorktown." The men seemed to be suffering measles, mumps and other illnesses common to new soldiers arriving in camp. Many of the soldiers had never been exposed to common childhood ailments, and many died. Of the two Mecklenburg companies stationed at Yorktown with the First North Carolina Volunteers, the Hornet's Nest Riflemen lost six men to disease, and the Charlotte Grays lost five men before their first six months of service was up. The *Fayetteville Observer* applauded the work of the ladies in Charlotte and encouraged the ladies in their town to take up the challenge of caring for the soldiers in the field.[28]

Later in July 1861, the Hospital Association morphed into the Soldiers Aid Society of Charlotte. Mrs. Sophia Myers was the president. Mrs. Ann Osborne reported after the war that the Soldiers Aid Society, containing sixty-five members, met three times a week. Wednesdays were devoted to sewing, "the ladies plying their needles, not in embroidery, but making uniforms, drawers, overcoats, shorts, haversacks, gloves, comforts, bed-ticks, pillows, and socks." There were dues of twenty-five cents per month, and ladies not attending the meetings were fined. "The first year our organization made 301 garments of which 207 was sent to the Montgomery Hospital in Virginia for the use of the North Carolina soldiers there." An advertisement in the newspaper asked the ladies to assemble at the Bulletin Building, at nine o'clock in the morning, with Mrs. Myers requesting "those who have sewing Machines to bring them." Many donated money to be used by the society. Benjamin Shepherd donated $50; "the coloured ladies of Charlotte" donated $25. Bessie Dewery, the society's secretary, thanked the contributors, writing, "Our country's cause is a common one with master and servant alike, and it behooves us all to…show the fanatics of the North that we of the South, regardless of color, stand as a unit to sustain and strengthen the arms of the soldiers of our glorious Confederacy."[29]

The year 1861 was known for the dissolution of the Union, start of the war, the capitulation of Fort Sumter and the battles of Big Bethel and Manassas, all Confederate victories. "I trust that the result of the Battle of Manassas will satisfy the Northern People that we are in earnest," wrote John Wilkes to his wife. "Sorrowful though it is that things have been carried to such a point that there is no hope for reconstruction." As sorrowful as events appeared, they only became dreadfully worse in 1862.[30]

Chapter 3
"We Will Never Disgrace Our Native County"

1862

While 1861 brought some Confederate victories, it also brought reverses as well. For North Carolinians, the loss of the Outer Banks stood paramount in the press. Union forces captured Confederate defenses in August and began planning further advances to the west as winter progressed. "The landing at Hatteras and capture of the Fort will bring the war to our doors with a vengeance," confided John Wilkes to his wife. "It begins to look as if all able men will have to buckle on their arms & drive the invaders back." January 1862 saw a Confederate defeat at Mill Springs, Kentucky; and in February, Roanoke Island, North Carolina, and Forts Henry and Donelson, Tennessee, were lost.[31]

Men in Charlotte went to the polls again on January 13, 1862, in what was billed the "most warmly contested election we have ever had." William Owens, the young lawyer who was already a Confederate veteran, defeated Dr. Henry Pritchard, 207 to 146, for the position of mayor. Owens only served a couple of weeks before rejoining the Confederate army as major of the Thirty-fourth North Carolina Troops. It appears that Robert Davidson served as mayor pro tem in Owens's absence.[32]

Owens and other new troops from the surrounding areas boarded the train at the Charlotte depot. These troop trains often consisted of boxcars fitted with plank seats or just boxcars or flatcars without seats. Lieutenant Joseph Hoyle, of Company F, Fifty-fifth North Carolina Troops, took the train from Lincolnton to Charlotte. He found his three hours "very disagreeable owning to a want of accommodations in seats." After waiting

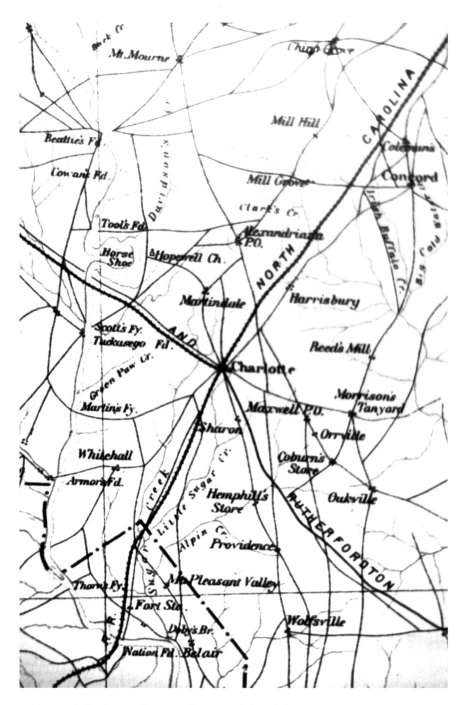

1863 map of Charlotte and surrounding area. *Author's Collection.*

in Charlotte for several hours, Hoyle and his company boarded a train for Raleigh. "We had excellent seats in this ride," he wrote to his wife back in Cleveland County.[33]

Traveling by rails was often dangerous. Soldiers rode on the tops of cars or played with the equipment; a popular pastime was removing the pin coupling the cars, forcing the trains to stop, back up and reconnect. This was all funny until some poor soldier fell off and was run over. Derailments and collisions were frequent. On February 18, about ten miles north of Charlotte, a freight train that had just left Charlotte collided with the express train coming from Salisbury, injuring several. The express train was loaded with Georgia and Alabama troops heading home on furlough. Colonel Thomas Judge, of the Fourteenth Alabama Infantry, fractured his leg in the incident, causing Judge to resign from the service several months later. Samuel Dean "had his ankle so badly crushed that amputation was necessary." Those injured were taken back to Elms's Hotel in Charlotte and treated by local doctors. Charlotte residents donated at least $120 for the care of the injured men.[34]

No other act by the Confederate Congress was as despised as the Conscription Act. The topic first arose in December 1861 but lacked support, with the compromise of a Furlough and Bounty Act granting all twelve-month enlistees a furlough home and a bounty if they would voluntarily reenlist. On February 20, the *Charlotte Daily Bulletin* came out in support of conscription. "We are decidedly in favor of that policy," wrote Editor Yates, "not only because it is the only equitable mode of procedure, but because it will relieve thousands who are desirous to fight in defence[sic] of our rights and institutions, but in consequence of family responsibility and other sacred obligation they do not feel justified in thrusting themselves forward as volunteers; but especially because an order of that sort will bring from their hiding places many mean, mercenary, and traveling speculators who never will take up arms in defence of the country unless forced to do." Jefferson Davis, realizing that the Furlough and Bounty Act had failed, submitted to Congress on March 28 a bill requiring that all white, able-bodied men between the ages of eighteen and thirty-five years old join the army for three years or the duration of the war. Men already serving had to reenlist for three additional years or the duration of the war.[35]

There were numerous exemptions in the Act. Workers in various industries, like manufacturing and shipbuilding, factory owners, miners, tanners, salt producers, postal workers, railroad employees, blacksmiths and mechanics were exempt. Those who owned or oversaw twenty or more slaves were also exempt. The bill also allowed a man to hire another as a substitute. One such case in Mecklenburg was that of James Kerr, who was forty-four years old when he was conscripted into Company F, Forty-ninth North Carolina Troops in August 1863. Kerr was discharged on December 11, 1863, after providing his son, James Kerr, as a substitute. The younger Kerr later died of wounds in a hospital in Richmond, Virginia, in May 1865. Advertisements for men to serve as substitutes often ran in local newspapers. The *Western Democrat* ran an ad in August 1862 that simply read: "Substitute Wanted: A substitute over forty-five years of age for which a fair price will be paid. Apply to Dr. E. Nye Hutchison at Charlotte or J[.]P. Henderson of Davidson College." Companies and regiments already in the process of organizing had until May 17 to complete their organization. Later, that date was pushed back until July 8 and then August 1. The act of conscription was an attempt to encourage enlistment by men who had otherwise been lukewarm in their military sentiments. These unwilling volunteers could elect their officers and collect a bounty just as the men who had enlisted in 1861 had done. Men who waited could do neither, and once they came in or were caught, they were often assigned to any understaffed regiment rather than having the opportunity to serve with friends and family. There were at least four companies from Mecklenburg County formed after the passage of the Act.[36]

Local residents had numerous reasons to be concerned for their fathers, brothers, husbands and sons in the Confederate army. Federal forces landed below New Bern on March 13 and, the following day, stormed the Confederate defenses. Confederate losses amounted to 578 killed, wounded or captured. Word traveled back, via a local man who witnessed part of the battle, that all of the Confederates had been killed. At Hopewell Church, home to many members of the Thirty-seventh North Carolina, the news arrived just before the service began. When asked about any of the soldiers, the man's response was: "I saw him fall; yes, they are all killed." According to a local historian, "One lady at Hopewell when she heard the news, fainted and had to be helped home." A telegram arrived about that time, stating that all of Captain Pott's company was well, but the people did not believe it. Later, they learned that there were few actual losses among local men. "No man knows what a battle is until he is in one," wrote Dr. John B. Alexander a few days after battle.[37]

New Bern was a Confederate loss, not only on the battlefield, but in camp equipment also. The Confederates were forced to abandon everything as they retreated. Charlotte citizens rallied to their aid. At a public meeting held on March 16, a committee was appointed "to solicit contributions of blankets, clothing, &c.," from local citizens to help the troops, who were "in a suffering condition." Local newspapers are full of accounts of ladies giving blankets, socks, shirts and even money to help with the needs of soldiers. These acts of benevolence continued for the rest of the war. In September 1861, the Sharon Ladies Soldiers Aid Society contributed many items, like blankets, bed ticks and pillows, coverlets, sheets and other items. In May 1862, the Soldiers Aid Society at Steele Creek donated blankets and socks, and also sent five pounds of wool, five yards of cotton drilling and three cuts of cotton yarn. These items were often deposited at Brown, Tate and Company's store in Charlotte. John Brown had agreed to serve as "general agent" for Mecklenburg County and was responsible for receiving and forwarding donated items.[38]

Often when these soldiers received the donated goods, they gathered and sent out resolutions of thanks like that passed by the Mecklenburg Rifles (Company I, Thirty-seventh North Carolina Troops) following the New Bern fiasco. Captain John Harrison chaired the committee, which sought to "express…our gratitude to the good citizens of Mecklenburg, for their prompt aid in this, our hour of need." Additionally, to try to protect their good names with the recent loss, they added "that as we have never turned our backs to the enemy until ordered-we will never disgrace our native county." This was more than just expressing loyalty to North Carolina or the Confederate cause. They were concerned about the reputation of old Mecklenburg.[39]

Charlotte people were presented another opportunity to help the Confederate cause. An article appeared in the *Western Democrat* on April 8, entitled "CHURCH BELLS WANTED." The Confederate Ordnance Bureau was seeking brass bells that could be melted down and recast into light artillery pieces. The bureau promised to replace the bells at the end of the war. A public meeting was called at the courthouse in Charlotte, with James Osborne as chairman. Those present moved to donate the town bell to the war effort, while at the same time, requesting that the various churches in the area also contribute their bells. Churches across the state answered the Confederate government's call. According to an essay written after the war, all five churches in Charlotte donated their bells to the war effort. The *Charlotte Daily Bulletin* reported on April 28 that Mayor Davidson had received notification from the government that the bells "tendered by several denominations in Charlotte" had been received and "that the cannon cast out the metal will be marked the Charlotte Battery, to be placed under charge of Capt. Brem." The Charlotte Artillery had been forced to abandon its guns as the New Bern defenses fell earlier that year.[40]

More industries were popping up in the Queen City. In March, prominent business leaders met at the courthouse to organize a "company for the manufacture of small arms and ordnance." Williamson Wallace, who was called upon to chair the meeting, introduced William Johnston to explain why they had gathered. Three different sites were proposed for the location of such a facility: "The angle of W.C. & Rutherford and Tennessee and Atlantic Railroads, the Rudisill Planing [sic] and Foundry, and Alexander's Machine Works." Those present subscribed over fifteen thousand dollars to the project and called for another

William Johnston. *North Carolina Museum of History.*

meeting. At a meeting near the end of March, James Irwin, A.B. Davidson, Williamston Wallace, James Davis, S.P. Alexander, Joseph Wilson and William Johnston were elected directors. Other backers were sought for the project, and in April 1862, a charter and bylaws were presented.[41]

Toward the end of March, various newspapers and political parties in North Carolina began to consider who should run for the governorship of the Old North State. John Ellis had been governor in May 1861 when North Carolina seceded from the Union. However, Ellis died on July 7, 1861, and was replaced by President of the Senate Henry T. Clark. North Carolina had no elected lieutenant governor at that time. Clark guided North Carolina through the early months of the war, helping to build the war effort and rushing Tar Heel soldiers into the Confederate army, but chose not to run in the regular election; North Carolina began looking for candidates for governor.

"Our readers will perceive," conveyed the *Western Democrat*, "that we have placed at the head of our columns the name of William Johnston, of the county of Mecklenburg, as the candidate for the office of Governor to whom, as a member of the Southern Rights party, we give our support." The forty-five-year-old Johnston was a graduate of the University of North Carolina, a lawyer and railroad president. He had represented Mecklenburg County in the secession convention in 1861 and, from May to September 1861, served as commissary general of North Carolina, with the rank of colonel. Johnston had little political experience. On accepting the nomination, he told the Charlotte crowd "that he had never been an office-seeker, but he felt highly complimented at being recommended by his fellow-citizens as a candidate for Governor, and if the duties of the office should devolve upon him he would endeavor to discharge the trust faithfully and for the good of the State and country." The *Fayetteville Observer* thought Johnston had "the reputation of being a man of integrity, ability and industry." Others were not so supportive. The Raleigh *Weekly Standard* wrote in March that Johnston was "an ultra and bitter partisan secessionist" and in July that he was "not at all qualified to manage the helm of State in a crisis like the present. He has been at the bar for more than twenty-five years, and has made no reputation beyond that of a County Court lawyer." Running against Johnston was Zebulon Baird Vance. The thirty-two-year-old Vance hailed from Buncombe County and had also attended the University of North Carolina. Vance practiced law in Asheville, served in the General Assembly and, in 1858, was elected to the United States Congress. After raising a company in Buncombe County, Vance was elected colonel of the Twenty-sixth North Carolina Troops, commanding the regiment at the battles of New Bern and Seven Days.[42]

Neither Johnston nor Vance actively campaigned in North Carolina. Vance was stationed in Virginia, and Johnston was increasingly busy running his railroad. The candidates relied greatly on the newspapers in the state to advance their platforms, with eleven newspapers backing Vance and ten siding with Johnston. Johnston was a member of the Confederate Party who supported Jefferson Davis and believed that war should be prosecuted until "the last extremity with no compromise with enemies, traitors, and tories." Vance and the Conservative Party believed that the war should continue, but that civil liberties should be protected at all cost. Soldiers in the field went to the polls before Tar Heel voters cast their ballots. Of the thirty-three regiments reported in the *Western Democrat* on August 21, Vance received 841 votes while 657 were cast for Johnston. Statewide, the election was not that close: 54,423 to 20,448. In Charlotte, 532 votes were cast for Johnston, while Vance gained 106. Henry Pritchard was elected to represent the county in the State Senate and J L. Brown in the Commons. A.J. Hood was elected over R.M. White for sheriff.[43]

While the debate over the next governor of North Carolina raged, the citizens of Charlotte worked with Confederate officials to establish their first hospital. According to an article in the *Charlotte Observer* written three decades after the war by Lily Long, "The first Hospital in Charlotte was established by the ladies, in a large building used as the wash-house for the Military Institute…Here all the arrangements were made for the care of the passing soldiers. Every day two members of the Hospital Association went there with supplies of all necessary articles, and gave their time and strength to nursing and caring for the men." Thomas Dewey, treasurer for the town of Charlotte, noted on July 7, 1862:

Zebulon Vance served as North Carolina governor, 1862–65. He met with Jefferson Davis in Charlotte in 1865. *North Carolina State Archives.*

> *During the past few days large numbers of wounded soldiers have passed through this place, who have had their wounds dressed and other wants attended to at the depot, the Mayor with a skillful Surgeon being in attendance on the arrival of the different trains, and our citizens have liberally supplied provisions for their refreshment in passing through. Buildings have been obtained near the Depot for the Hospital and will be in readiness in a few days for the reception of those who may be compelled to lie over in their passage through Charlotte.*

A week later, the ladies of Charlotte were congratulated on being "more than hospitable. They have kept a table spread at the depot on the arrival of trains especially and exclusively for soldiers…they have supplied the war worn and wounded every nourishment for the body." The ladies, the mayor and his unnamed surgeon were undoubtedly busy. The Seven Days battles near Richmond raged the last week of June, producing 20,000 Confederate causalities. The 15,758 wounded quickly overpowered the hospital facilities in Richmond, and wounded soldiers were sent to other hospitals or furloughed home.[44]

One of the dead was Colonel Charles Lee of the Thirty-seventh North Carolina Troops, former instructor at the Military Institute. On June 30, Lee and his regiment were battling the Federals at Frayser's Farm when he was killed by a cannon blast. The *North Carolina Whig* sang his praises with, "Thus has died upon the altar of our country one of nature's noblemen, none who knew him but to love him, a gentleman, a scholar and a true soldier fallen. May his memory ever remain fresh in our hearts, his monument a nation's gratitude. Peace to his ashes." Lee's remains were returned to Charlotte, where he was laid to rest in the Oakwood Cemetery. All of the stores in Charlotte were closed on the day of his funeral.[45]

In mid-July, the Confederate government took charge of the hospital in Charlotte. In both the North and the South, wayside hospitals were established to provide food, rest and minor medical care for soldiers in transit to or from their assigned posts. In Charlotte, the facility was designated Wayside Hospital No. 4. Richard Gregory, a Greensboro native, graduate of the Medical Department of New York University and former United States army doctor, was assigned as post doctor (or contract doctor) probably in June 1862. Gregory asked the ladies of Charlotte and the surrounding area to supply old sheets, pillow slips, counterpanes and lint, along with "any delicacies, such as would gratify and be suitable for the sick and wounded" to be left in his office.[46]

A couple of days later, Gregory listed some of the items that had already been donated: surgical sponges by Drs. Hutchison and Scarr, one gallon of brandy and one wash basin by Dr. Elias, six chairs by Robert Davidson, two bottles of wine by H.C. Mark & Company and thirty-six yards of fabric by Drucker and Heilbrun.[47]

Along with a wayside hospital, the Confederate government established in March 1862 a branch of the Medical Purveyor's Department in Charlotte under Virginia surgeon Marion Howard. In early July, Howard advertised a list of medicinal herbs, barks and roots that the medical department was seeking and the proffered prices. All herbs had to "be clean and well dried." Sassafras pith brought $5.00 a pound, the highest of any herb on the list, while Indian Turnip brought just 10¢ per pound. Other herbs sought included Skunk Cabbage, White Oak bark, May Apple, Blackberry root and Butterfly Weed. These items were then transformed into medicine at a laboratory established at the North Carolina Military Institute in Charlotte. In June, Howard requisitioned a mortar and pestle and later advertised that he needed bottles and vials. Quart wine (Claret) bottles brought $1.00 per dozen, while quart castor oil bottles were 75¢ per dozen.[48]

The Confederate government also set up a quartermaster's department, under the command of Captain R.J. Echols. In September 1862, the department advertised that it was seeking fifty thousand pounds of scrap iron.[49]

Charlotte continued to grow and expand. In late 1861, local residents established the North Carolina Powder Manufacturing Company, with Sidney Davis as president. This facility was quite possibly the first in the state after the start of the war. Offices were established on the corner of Tryon and Fourth Streets, and construction began on the plant in the Tuckaseegee Ford area in the spring of 1862. The main building was a "stone structure at least 35 x 10 feet, no windows, no chimney, and just a single door." The mill employed local men who had been exempt from Confederate service and slaves or free persons of color. In November 1862, the company published its desire to purchase "10,000 White Oak and Chestnut Staves" to hold gunpowder, along with "110 Tons of Tobacco Stems."[50]

Local companies advertised items that had come through Federal naval blockades along the coast. Kahnweiler and Brothers advertised English hoop skirts, brown and black English cloth, French kid gloves and English shirts for men. Hilker and Rucks had oilcloth coats and also sold oilcloth by the yard. Robert Shaw advertised 1,500 pounds of English ball shoe thread.[51]

Wartime Charlotte's most influential industry also arrived in 1862: the Confederate Naval Yard. In 1861, the Confederate government concentrated most of its ship building industry in the major port cities of the South. Many of these cities fell in 1862: Nashville in February, Jacksonville in March, New Orleans in April and Pensacola and Norfolk in May. With the possible loss of the naval facility in Norfolk, officials began to look for a more secure location to manufacture naval-related equipment. According to Jane Wilkes, wife of businessman John Wilkes, two Confederate naval officers who knew her husband from the United States Navy came to Charlotte to explore the area. Wilkes showed them a piece of property he had recently acquired on East Trade Street. The agents found the property suitable and agreed to purchase it, while at the same time leasing the Mecklenburg Iron Works. The Queen City offered an important rail connection to both Virginia and South Carolina. When it became apparent that Norfolk would soon close, "a number of machines, tools, such as lathes, planing [sic] machines, and one small steam hammer, were hurriedly shipped to Charlotte" via the railroad, according to one early history. "A large quantity of material and coke ovens, foundry and machine shops were erected," recalled Jane Wilkes after the war. "A wooden landing stage was built from the yard to the railroad for convenience in loading and unloading." From Tredegar Iron Works came a "Nasmyth steam hammer, used for making propeller shafts and other heavy work." It took several months for the work to be completed, but by the end of the year, the establishment was in full operation. The location of the yard in Charlotte brought a flurry of activity. William Johnston rented a store to Confederate

This marker was placed on East Trade Street in 1910 to mark the area where the Confederate Naval Yard was located during the war. The marker has since disappeared. *University of North Carolina–Charlotte.*

officials, J.M. Howell sold the navy goat skins, William Flemming sold wheel hubs and Thomas Dewey sold real estate. By July 14, over twenty-seven thousand pounds of pig iron had been delivered. Another twenty-four thousand pounds arrived by the end of the month. Surprisingly, the appropriation form for October 1862 was written on United States Navy forms with the "U" crossed out and a "C" handwritten above it.[52]

Commanders at the Navy Yard seem to have changed often during the first few weeks of operations. Samuel Barron appeared in command in August 1862, though he seems to have been replaced by Commander Richard Page in September. There were scores of men from the naval yard in Norfolk who transferred to Charlotte. Bartlett Brown, Lee Wallace and John Davis were all veterans of the Third Virginia Infantry. They had been detailed to work at the Gosport Naval Yard in early 1862 and then transferred to Charlotte; they brought their families along. Housing was at a premium by the end of the war.[53]

One of the early refugees in Charlotte was Fannie Downing. She moved to Charlotte in 1862, possibly after the death of her husband. Downing was a poet, sometimes penning pieces under the name Viola.[54]

The changes in town led to new ordinances going into effect by the end of 1862. In November, it became illegal to sell "spirituous liquors" under five gallons within the town limits or within one mile of Charlotte. The treasurer was responsible for issuing refunds to those who had valid permits. Druggists could fill prescriptions, but individuals caught with alcohol were fined one hundred dollars for each offense. The commissioners proposed in December, due to an outbreak of small pox, to ban all rural slaves from entering Charlotte, unless they were on special business and had written permission. Those caught on the streets were subject to arrest and whipping, complicating the usual practice of giving slaves the week off between Christmas and New Year's Day to visit and celebrate the holidays.[55]

The Soldiers Aid Society continued to work. On November 11, the group sponsored a concert at Theloar's Hall. Admission was one dollar, with the proceeds going toward charitable work. The ladies also continued to volunteer at the Wayside Hospital, trying to help traveling soldiers. At times, the *Charlotte Daily Bulletin* ran work assignments for the next few days. On November 26, Mrs. Sinclair and Mrs. Carson were assigned; on Thursday, Mrs. C.C. Lee and Mrs. Captain Lowe; and on Friday, Mrs. Overman and Miss Patey Watson. On Monday, November 3, the duty fell to Mrs. Lucas and Mrs. Wilkes; Tuesday, Mrs. C. Elma and Mrs. E. Britton; Thursday, Mrs. Coldiron and Mrs. John Howie; and, on Friday, Mrs. N. Johnston and Mrs. R. Surwell. Just how many of these ladies were, like Mrs. Lee, still grieving the loss of a husband at the cruel hands of war is unknown. She was undoubtedly not the only one.[56]

Chapter 4

"The War May Be Prolonged Indefinitely"

1863

In many ways, the war stayed out of Charlotte and Mecklenburg County. No army came through raiding and plundering, and no pitched battles produced tens of thousands of dead and wounded within its confines. Yet the war was very real. Men volunteered to go and fight in the army. Many did not return, and some returned only to be buried in one of the local cemeteries. Wartime industry expanded the commercial district of Charlotte, while bringing hundreds of new people, laborers and other refugees to the Queen City.

Anyone needing a reminder of the war simply needed to visit the Wayside hospital. December 1862 began with ten men sick or convalescent. Thirty-nine passed through. Twenty-six of these were wounded men, undoubtedly from the recent Fredericksburg battle. Others had typhoid fever, measles, pneumonia or syphilis. January 1, 1863, saw seven sick men and three convalescent. Twenty-one were added through the month. Ten were gunshot victims, probably also Fredericksburg causalities. Three others had pneumonia, and one each had scarlet fever, debility, chronic diarrhea and other fevers. For February, the hospital still reported ten present. Twenty-seven had been treated, two for gunshot wounds and eight with pneumonia.[57]

Locals were almost silent on learning of the Emancipation Proclamation. On January 13, the *Western Democrat* ran a piece quoting from and elaborating on an article from the New York *Herald*, stating that the "slaves taken from our citizens during the war will have to be accounted for at its end, either by restoration or indemnity." A week earlier, that paper had reported on

Constructed in 1845, the Mecklenburg County Courthouse in Charlotte was the site of numerous public gatherings during the war. *Public Library of Charlotte-Mecklenburg County.*

the annual hiring day, when slaves with skilled labor specialties were hired out for the year. In a jocular way the paper wrote, "Judging from the way negroes hired and sold here on the 1st of January, we suppose nobody in this section is afraid of Old Abe's proclamation." There was no noticeable rise in the advertisements for runaways in any of the Charlotte-based newspapers.

Defining the slave-master relationship in wartime Charlotte is challenging. Dr. John Alexander wrote after the war: "The negroes were well treated and cared for; in fact, there was too much money value wrapped up in them to be treated otherwise. The best Physicians in the state were employed to wait upon them." In 1861, Daniel Hill, writing to his publisher in Philadelphia, confided, "The few slaves I own, I love, and I know they are devoted to me. But I would give them up, if it were right, at any moment." Finding documentation on the thoughts of local slaves during the wartime years has proved elusive. In December 1862, the General Assembly passed, after considerable debate, an act allowing the governor to "impress" slaves to work on coastal fortifications. Owners were to be compensated for their work: fifteen dollars per month for "ordinary hands" and "one dollar per day for mechanics"; they were compensated if the laborers "shall escape to the enemy, or be captured or killed by them." One-tenth of the slaves in Mecklenburg County were called out to meet on April 9. "Would it not be better for the slaveholders of each county to club together and employ some one of their number well acquainted with the management of negroes to go with the hands furnished and superintend and oversee them?" groused the *Western Democrat.* A year later, a call went out for sixty-five slaves to work on the railroad to Statesville; in 1865, there was a request "to furnish Negroes to blockade the roads and fords leading to this place from the south." It took just two days to secure three hundred slaves for the job.[58]

"Runaways," was the headline of a front-page article in June 1863. "Portions of this county have been infested for some time past with runaway negroes." Several were captured, reported the *Western Democrat,* adding that "owners of these negroes are humane masters, and nothing but devilishness or improper influences brought to bear on the negroes, could induce them to runaway." The *Democrat* actually went a step further in detailing the problem, writing "In certain portions of the country runaway negroes and deserters are committing depredations and have become a terror to the neighborhood." Early that year, the paper had reported a barn-burning incident in northern Mecklenburg County. "There are bad men prowling about throughout the county, doing all the harm they can." Not only were some of these "bad men" runaway slaves, but some of them were also runaway soldiers.[59]

Desertion was a problem for all of the armies in the field, North and South. While furloughs home were given to some men, not enough were issued to satisfy the volunteer soldiers. So they resorted to leaving of their own accord. According to the Articles of War, the penalty for desertion was death. However, this execution was seldom prescribed. In January 1863, Governor Vance asked the general assembly to make aiding deserters a crime, while at the same time issuing a proclamation granting clemency to soldiers who were absent without leave if they voluntarily returned to their regiments. Private Osborne Fincher of Company F, Forty-ninth North Carolina Troops was probably one soldier who took up Vance on his offer. The nineteen-year-old farmer deserted from the army on August 18, 1862, while stationed in Petersburg. He returned to his regiment on January 15, 1863. Local newspapers were rife with advertisements for the capture of deserters. Captain David Maxwell advertised in February for the apprehension of Private James Blunt, a thirty-four-year-old Mecklenburg County farmer who had deserted from the hospital in Kinston in May 1862. A description of

Blunt was given, including a scar on his leg caused by a gunshot wound. "He is supposed to be lurking in the vicinity of Morrow's Turnout," wrote Maxwell, who offered thirty dollars for Blunt's return to the camp of the Thirty-fifth North Carolina Troops.[60]

Not all crimes were committed by slaves or deserters. At one session of the Mecklenburg County court, John Mincey, "a white man," stood trial and was found guilty for robbing "a Jewish Rabbi at the Charlotte Hotel," stealing his pocketbook and watch. Mincey's punishment was "thirty-nine lashes, immediately, remain in Jail three months, and then received thirty-

Local businessman William Myers served the Confederacy in various roles during the war and later donated the property for what is now Johnson C. Smith University. *Public Library of Charlotte-Mecklenburg County.*

nine lashes again." Whipping was a common punishment for a variety of crimes. Around that same time, the smokehouse of the Reverend Burwell was robbed of three sacks of flour and "other articles."[61]

Huntersville resident Amanda McRaven warned her husband, David, a prison guard at Salisbury, "I heard that [name unknown] had taken up with one of them bad women at Charlotte and was doing no good [.] dont you forget your self and go among them filthy wemen[.] I have more confidence in you than that."[62]

If runaway slaves, thieves and deserters were not enough trouble, many residents complained of Yankee prisoners running loose through the city. It seemed that when prisoners arrived in Charlotte, they were "allowed… to run over the city and communicate, freely, with a certain class of our population." The paper called on elected leaders to put in place laws or regulations that would "effectually suppress…such unwarrantable privileges, for the miserable band of thieves, incendiaries, murderers and despoilers of Southern maidens…captured on their hellish expeditions, are not entitled to any privileges nor countenance…by Southern men." Sergeant Leonard Ferguson, Fifty-seventh Pennsylvania Infantry, passed through Charlotte about a year later. Ferguson was captured during the Wilderness Campaign and eventually imprisoned at Andersonville, Georgia. In his diary, Ferguson made no mention of roaming the streets, simply noting that his train arrived in Charlotte at 6:00 p.m. on July 7, where he drew "6 Hard Tack and a little Meat for Two days rations." They were on the cars again and heading for Columbia by 3:00 a.m.[63]

Mecklenburg County was not the only county to wrestle with the problems of deserters. It was actually much worse in places like Wilkes County, where a band of 1,100 draft evaders and deserters marched into Wilkesboro. Part of the problem was that North Carolina Supreme Court Chief Justice Richmond Pearson had ruled that conscription was illegal and that Vance had no authority to arrest deserters or conscripts using the state's militia. So Vance countered by forming a separate organization in July: the Guard for Home Defence, commonly referred to as the Home Guard. All able-bodied white men between the ages of eighteen and fifty, including those exempt from Confederate service, like militia officers, comprised the Home Guard. On August 22, citizens liable for home guard duty gathered at the militia district mustering grounds to organize themselves into companies. August 29 was designated the day for the officers of these companies to assemble and elect a battalion commander. Not all districts in the county complied, and a second call went out, with orders for the men in Mallard Creek and Crab Orchard to meet on September 19 to organize. All companies were requested to send to headquarters the number of men they contained, along with the number and type of firearms and the supply of ammunition on hand. Thomas Brem, who had commanded a company of artillery until resigning due to old age (he was forty-six at the time), was commissioned lieutenant colonel of the Sixty-third Battalion, Guard for Home Defence, on September 14, 1863. Brem ordered a battalion-wide drill and inspection in Charlotte on Saturday, October 8. Individual companies were required to drill every Saturday, along with making out returns of men enrolled in their companies.[64]

Another topic of debate in the summer and fall of 1863 was the peace movement. William Holden began in June 1863 to call for peace through the pages of the *North Carolina Standard.* Holden believed that the only solution "to arrest this awful evil" was to demand peace. That peace, however, had to "preserve the rights of the sovereign States and the institutions of the

South." Holden believed that the "two governments are so inflamed by the war spirit, and so intent on mere physical triumphs, that unless the people of the two sections rise up and demand…to close the war…the war may be prolonged indefinitely." Holden's words fanned a hidden ember. Between July 3 and September 9, 1863, there were nearly one hundred peace rallies held in North Carolina. While a few of these were held in the eastern and western sections of the state, the vast majority, almost 80 percent, took place in the central counties. Holden publicized many of these gatherings and encouraged others to speak. Charlotte citizens did speak out. At a public meeting held at the courthouse on September 1, they gathered and adopted a set of resolutions. Yet instead of supporting Holden's cry of "the Constitution as it is, the Union as it was," the same cry of the Northern Peace Democrats, the Mecklenburg resolutions wholeheartedly expressed confidence in the Confederate government. John Walker chaired the meeting, and Joseph Wilson the resolution committee. While the committee met, North Carolina Confederate senator George Davis spoke. On returning, the mass of people agreed with the resolutions, that "the citizens of Mecklenburg county have unabated confidence in the justice of the cause," that the common soldiers in the field had "acquitted themselves like heroes, determined to be free" and that while the people of Mecklenburg desired peace, the "Peace Meetings" currently being held were "ill-timed" and had been "stimulated by a few disloyal and wicked men…creating discord and depression among our people." The resolutions were "unanimously and enthusiastically adopted" by everyone in attendance.[65]

Charlotte and its population continued to expand and to suffer hardships and losses. The naval works grew, adding a third steam hammer, this one from Pensacola. At one time, the yard employed around 1,100 men. Page was replaced by Captain George Hollis, who was replaced by Lieutenant Catesby Jones. Engineer H. Ashton Ramsey served briefly, before being replaced by Jones. Offices for the naval yard were on the corner of A and Trade Streets. Paymaster John Johnson was stationed at the old mint building. In November 1863, John Brooke, commander of the Confederate Ordnance and Hydrography department, gave this description of the naval facilities. The works had been "improved by the addition of machinery manufactured there…The foundry facilities have been increased by the addition of flasks, patterns, and a new cupola furnace…The smithery has been increased, and the building extended to receive a new steam hammer…The gun carriage and block shops are finished and in operation. Two coke ovens have been erected. The laboratory continues in successful operation."[66]

Jefferson Davis, President of the Confederate States of America, passed through Charlotte several times during the war. *Library of Congress.*

In mid-1863, the Confederate government sought to develop more wartime industries in Charlotte. A Sulphuric Acid Works, a part of the Nitre and Mining Bureau, was established near Charlotte, under the control of William Schirmer. The Acid Works provided several different components for the Confederate war machine; in mid-1863, it procured the materials to manufacture saltpeter, one of the key components in gunpowder. Local residents were encouraged to examine the grounds around their homes and alert Schirmer if the substance was found. Professor William Winston arrived in late 1863 to examine the Rudisell Mine. Soon thereafter, Winston was serving as bureau agent, and the facility was manufacturing sulphuric acid to use in the wet cell batteries that powered the telegraph and in the process of manufacturing fulminate of mercury, used in percussion caps for muskets. Daniel Hill estimated that the sulphuric acid chambers yielded four thousand to five thousand pounds a month.[67]

There was also much tragedy. Major battles like Chancellorsville, Virginia, in May and Gettysburg, Pennsylvania, in July, robbed the community of scores of men killed, wounded and captured. "To our mind," chronicled the *Western Democrat,* Gettysburg "was one of the wisest, grandest and most imposing schemes ever conceived by the mind of man." Yet many a Charlotte mother, wife and child mourned the loss of a Southern soldier boy, slain on the outskirts of the Pennsylvania town. Earlier in the year, several miles from the heart of the Queen City, the gunpowder mill exploded. According to one of the workers, they were cleaning the mill when it exploded. The May 23 blast killed four: John Lee Jr., George Hutchison, Christopher Ounce and superintendent Charles Klepelburge. Another workman, John Ochler, later died. The explosion was felt several miles away. In September, the Mansion House, a local hotel, caught fire, destroying much of the building. "The hotel was full of boarders," it was reported, "many of them refugees from their homes. The loss and inconvenience to them is very great."[68]

One other tragic element in Charlotte society deteriorated each passing day: the plight of the poor. Food prices continued to rise, while the pay of the soldiers in the army did not. At least one, possibly two, different relief organizations were formed in 1863. One organization was the Donation Association of the town of Charlotte, with Samuel Harris as president, charged with buying provisions for the needy. By November 18, over $17,000 had been subscribed. The other group was the Laboring Man's Relief Association. By November 23, over $18,000 had been pledged to this group. As 1863 closed and a new year dawned, conditions only became worse.[69]

Chapter 5

"Take Courage and Press On to Victory"

1864

The year 1864 seemed like one endless military campaign. In January, the Confederates attempted to regain New Bern and Plymouth, capturing the latter in April. May brought the opening of the Overland Campaign to the north of Richmond, followed by the Petersburg Campaign to the south of Richmond. In Georgia, Federal general William Sherman launched his campaign to capture Atlanta.

In late summer and early fall 1863, eastern Tennessee, with its vital North-South railroad, fell to Federal forces. Now, the shortest link between Deep South cities like Georgia's Atlanta and Augusta was through Charlotte. This greatly overtaxed local resources, especially when large troop movements occurred. In September 1863, the bulk of Longstreet's Corps passed through the town, en route to Chickamauga. Due to gauge difference, every soldier, crate, supply and prisoner had to disembark from the cars of the North Carolina Railroad and climb aboard or be loaded onto the cars of the Charlotte and South Carolina Railroad to continue on the journey south. In March 1864, the Confederate government assumed control of the railroads, limiting passenger service to one daily train. All others were devoted to government freight. The editor of the *Western Democrat* complained in mid-April that there had been no mail for three or four days due to the transport of provisions for the Army of Northern Virginia.[70]

Both government and private freight backed up at the depots of Charlotte. In April, a group of local women, probably gaining inspiration from an 1863 female-led raid in Salisbury, "liberated" from the depot twenty-three sacks of meal bound for a distillery in Iredell County.[71]

One Federal prisoner, a member of the First Rhode Island Cavalry, passed through Charlotte in March 1864, "where we stayed one night. About four o'clock in the morning, three men ran through the guard, who fired at them. This aroused the whole camp, and the rebels, fearing we would all escape, ordered us to lie down. One man, somewhat deaf, did not hear the order, but remained standing, when the guard shot him through the head. One other man died that night, and both were buried in one grave." Other breakouts were more successful. In May, the *Western Democrat* advised local citizens to be on the lookout for eleven escaped Yankee prisoners: "Besides, it is dangerous to have a set of villainous yankees prowling through our country."[72]

Charlotte's First Presbyterian Church hosted the annual meeting of Presbyterian Churches in 1864 and numerous veteran gatherings after the war. *Public Library of Charlotte-Mecklenburg County.*

The railroad also brought delegates for the annual meeting of the Presbyterian Church of the Confederate States. There were about sixty delegates from seven different states. Reverend John Wilson, of Georgia, was moderator. Telegrams received during the sessions announced the Confederate army's success over the Federals in the Wilderness in Virginia. On the evening of Tuesday, May 10, Reverend Beverly Lacy addressed the crowd for about two hours on the life of Stonewall Jackson. One attendee considered the crowd "one of the largest audiences we have ever seen assembled in Charlotte." Lacy had served as Jackson's chaplain before Stonewall's death.[73]

Some churches were hard hit during the war years. The First Baptist Church in Charlotte struggled to stay afloat. It took a quorum of five male members to conduct business, and seldom could they be found. The Sunday School, "perhaps the most encouraging feature of the church" prior to the war, was reduced to one teacher and one student. Because the church could not meet his salary, the pastor, Dr. R.H. Griffin, attempted to resign in 1861. He was persuaded to remain, and the arrival of workers from Norfolk for the Naval Yard, along with refugees from other parts of the South, breathed new life into the church. St. Peter's Episcopal Church fared a little better. The members were able to raise money during the war to purchase and import prayer books and Bibles from overseas. In early 1864, John Wilkes and Rev. George Everhart, rector of St. Peter's, started "The Protestant Episcopal Church Publishing Association," which published tracts for Confederate soldiers; titles included "Fragments for the Sick," "Prayers for the Sick and Wounded," "The Doubting Christian Encouraged" and "Profane Swearing."[74]

A year earlier, the Confederate Congress had passed its first comprehensive tax laws. One section required certain professional men to pay a fee for a license. Tobacconists, livery stable keepers, cattle brokers, butchers, bakers, apothecaries, photographers, lawyers, physicians and confectioners all had to pay $50. Bankers were required to pay $500. Another section of the tax law was referred to as tax-in-kind. Farmers, after keeping a certain percentage for their own consumption, were assessed with a debt of one-tenth of their agricultural production. Local agents, who were despised, collected wheat, oats, corn, rice, potatoes, fodder, sugar, cotton, wool, tobacco and rye. These items were then sent to local, and then regional, collection points to be forwarded to the army. The program was highly unpopular, and many citizens gathered frequently to denounce the measure, along with other threats to state sovereignty and personal freedoms. Captain S.M. Finger was the officer in charge of the Eighth Congressional District in North Carolina. All items except corn and bacon had to be turned in by April 1. Many of the lower and lower-middle class North Carolinians had never before been required to pay a tax, and for those in this demographic who practiced only subsistence farming, the program literally took food from needy families. "There are too many irresponsible men running over the country impressing, or threatening to impress," wrote the *Western Democrat.* Many found the agents incompetent and thought they should be back in the

William Wood Holden edited a newspaper in Raleigh, ran for governor in 1864, led the Peace Movement and was appointed military governor of North Carolina in 1865. *North Carolina State Archives.*

army. William Patterson, a Mecklenburg County farmer, grew 1,834 bushels of corn, and after subtracting several bad bushels, owed the government 128 bushels, valued at $236. He grew 1,230 pounds of cotton, owing the government 123 pounds with a value of $123. In the end, the people in North Carolina contributed more than any other state to this despised form of taxation.[75]

Toward the end of 1863, Charlotte citizens went to the polls to elect a new mayor: Samuel Harris. Harris had the town ordinances compiled and published in local papers. He also "commenced…to effect a revolution in certain quarters and among a certain class" of the population. In August 1864, the polls opened again. Vance was running for reelection, this time against newspaper editor William Holden, whom Vance handily defeated. In Charlotte, 701 votes were cast: 700 for Vance and one for Holden. W.M. Grier defeated John Young for the state senate, and John Brown and E.C. Grier won seats in the House of Commons.[76]

Work continued at the hospital in town. In addition to the Wayside Hospital, the Confederate government established a general hospital in July 1862, naming Richard Gregory surgeon in charge. Gregory oversaw both the Wayside Hospital and the General Hospital. Most of the major Southern cities, like Wilmington, Raleigh and Salisbury, had General Hospitals. Charlotte's General Hospital was originally known as No. 10, but sometime in early 1864, the designation was changed to No. 11. At some point, Confederate authorities constructed a five-hundred-bed building at the fair grounds. In June 1864, Charlotte resident Robert Gibbon was transferred to Charlotte to take charge of the hospital. Gibbon started the war as surgeon of the Twenty-eighth North Carolina Troops before being assigned as a brigade surgeon. There was another Confederate surgeon in Charlotte: Dr. Charles Williamson was listed as naval post surgeon for the various Confederate troops stationed in town. He had his office at the "Naval Store" on South Tryon.[77]

Naval Yard commander Richard Page was promoted to brigadier general March 1 and assigned to command the outer defenses of Mobile Bay in Alabama. On his departure, the naval employees formed and marched Page to the station where he addressed the crowd. "No man will with more ability," commented one citizen, "and gallantry meet the demands of his country in any responsibility." The Works continued to manufacture carriages for heavy guns, along with propeller shafts for ironclads and mines (torpedoes) for rivers. However, there were severe labor shortages. New base commander H. Ashton Ramsey reported on May 5 that some of the "most important tools are idle a large portion of the time for want of mechanics." Those employees who were present "are working night and on Sunday and still are not able to fill orders for munitions of war as is desired." Ramsey reported that the ironclad CSS *Virginia*, stationed in Richmond, was ready for deployment, save for gun carriages and projectiles that would be produced at the Charlotte facility. He then provided a list of needed

Robert Gibbon served as surgeon in the Twenty-eighth North Carolina Troops and, toward the end of the war, as chief of the Charlotte area hospitals. *Author's Collection.*

Refugees, as portrayed here in this drawing from *Harper's Weekly*, were an ongoing problem in Charlotte throughout the war.

employees: mechanics, blacksmiths, gun-carriage makers, block makers, a pattern maker, coppersmith and molders. An abundant supply of workers never came.[78]

A call for even more troops went out in 1864. In February, the third Conscription Act was passed by the Confederate Congress, creating a reserve force by expanding the age of conscription. Boys between seventeen and eighteen constituted a junior reserve, while those between forty-five and fifty made up a senior reserve. These reserves took on tasks like guarding railroad bridges and depots, freeing up regular soldiers for frontline duty. Portions of what became Company B, Second North Carolina Junior Reserves, came from Mecklenburg County and were under the command of Rowan County's William Overman. Mustered into service on May 24, 1864, they fought at the battle of Bentonville in March 1865. Notices also went out to the captains of various militia companies, ordering them to gather men of Senior Reserve age on May 6 in Charlotte to form companies. What became Company G, Fourth North Carolina Senior Reserves began in May and June 1864, with Robert McNeely elected captain. Both of these companies removed even more men from a society already depleted by voluntary enlistment and conscription. In the Senior Reserves company, Lieutenant John M. Strong was a doctor; Daniel Asbury, a chemist; William Carrol, a cooper; J.K. Caruthers and E.P. Cochren, blacksmiths; and John Oehler, William Noles and Thomas Hannon, shoemakers; along with scores of farmers.[79]

Late September brought about yet another military organization. The state created the First Regiment, North Carolina Detailed Men. These were soldiers who worked in various wartime industries supporting the Confederacy. There were three companies from Charlotte: Company D, under the command of Captain William Paisley; Company E, under the command of Philip Whisnant; and Company F, under Captain William Brown. Abraham Mayer and William Sorey were both hospital stewards in Charlotte, and both served in Company D as lieutenants. This regiment could be activated by the governor in an emergency.[80]

Lieutenant Colonel Brem and the Sixty-third Battalion, North Carolina Home Guard, were still actively working in the area. In September, Brem took portions of his battalion into neighboring counties, capturing eight or nine deserters in Union County and one each in Anson, Stanley and Cabarrus counties. Orders soon came for the division of the home guard into three classes that the governor could call out for duty. To facilitate this, Brem called the home guard together and downsized, going from five companies to three. The First Class company was under the command of

Captain Richard Blythe; Captain Robinson commanded the Second Class company; and Captain Thomas Gluyas the Third Class. Blythe and the forty-six men in his company, along with Brem and his staff, were ordered to Goldsboro in mid-October, for thirty days of service.[81]

Charlotte witnessed the passage of many important Confederate leaders during the war years. Confederate vice president Alexander Stephens was in town on June 17, 1863, speaking for an hour at the Masonic House. Famed cavalry commander John H. Morgan passed through in December 1863. Local citizens donated four thousand dollars to help him organize a new cavalry force. Raphael Semmes, captain of the CSS *Alabama*, addressed a crowd at the courthouse in January 1864 and was "enthusiastically received." Jefferson Davis passed through on several different occasions, including in January 1863. He was again in town on September 21, 1864, speaking in the rain to a crowd gathered at the depot. After being introduced by William Johnston, Davis spoke for fifteen or twenty minutes, reminding the people of their ancestors, who had written the Mecklenburg Declaration of Independence and defied the British, calling on the deserter to return to his regiment and the people to have faith and "take courage and press on to victory."[82]

In less than a year, Davis returned to Charlotte, his cry of "take courage and press on to victory" just a fleeting hope.

Chapter 6

"Oh! When Will the Good Old Peaceful Times of '60 Return?"

1865

Atlanta and Savannah were lost; Richmond and Petersburg, besieged; Columbia, Charleston and Wilmington destined for imminent capitulation. For Charlotte's citizens, 1865 dawned as bleak as the winter winds pouring down the Appalachian Mountains.

"Terrible Conflagration," read the *Western Democrat* on January 10, 1865. A fire broke out in the early morning hours of January 7 in a Quartermaster's depot office. The wind carried the flames from a small building to the passenger shed, then to warehouses used by the Confederate Quartermaster's Department, finally consuming part of the depot. In the government warehouses were "over 23,000 sacks of corn and oats, 1,900 sacks of flour, 160 hogsheads of sugar, besides blankets, soldiers clothing, leather" and other items. Departmental papers were burned, along with a great number of bales of cotton and private baggage. Several thousand bushels of grain owned by Tredegar Iron Works in Richmond, awaiting shipment north, were consumed, contributing to the Confederacy's demise. The newspaper pronounced the fire "rather strange, to say the least." Local post commander, Colonel William Hoke, reported the loss to his commander later that day. The event was so important, and the loss so great to the struggling Confederate army, that it only took two days for Federal general-in-chief U.S. Grant to learn of it.[83]

Charlotte was packed to overflowing with refugees. Some were simply traveling through, like Confederate general Joseph E. Johnston and famed diarist Mary Chestnut, traveling on to Lincolnton. A Georgian, Dr. Abner

Camp Exchange was just one of the names for the Federal prison in Charlotte, which existed for only a few days. *Harvard University.*

McGarity, wrote his wife in January from Charlotte, waiting for a connection north: "Women are traveling all over the country in cars. There are more men at all the Depots and Cities than have been since the war commenced. Thousands of them have given up." Others were seeking sanctuary in the Queen City. "It is almost….impossible to obtain shelter for those already here," wrote one newspaper. Since Charlotte was so crowded, new refugees were advised to seek asylum in the country "or to go to some place other than Charlotte." Post Commander Hoke soon issued an order for all non-Charlotte citizens to report to his office to register. The problem was compounded by the arrival of one hundred ladies who had been working at the Columbia treasury bureau.[84]

Everyone was suffering. In 1861, a pound of bacon retailed for twenty-five cents. In 1865, that same pound of bacon cost $4.50. James Davis recalled that during the latter part of the war, his granaries were frequented so often by soldiers' relatives that the trip was called "going down to Egypt." They often came "in large companies, a soldier's wife or daughter driving a one-horse wagon, sometimes an ox, or a mule; and none turned away without a load." Mayor Harris called on people outside Charlotte to supply wood for the winter to the "destitute families, women and children" in town. The *Western Democrat* noted on February 21 that "within the last few days the price of provisions has advanced alarmingly in this market."

Local citizens were now paying what the newspapers from Richmond had advertised as the going rates. A month later, they noted that "seeds of all kind are scarce" and that the weather had not been conducive to planting. Even the Gas Works in Charlotte was out of resin, cut off by the advance of a Federal force in eastern North Carolina. Citizens and refugees alike were now subject to the "flickering flame of a tallow candle." One resident lamented "Oh! when will the good old peaceful times of '60 return," a sentiment doubtless felt by many.[85]

Columbia, South Carolina, fell to Federal forces on February 17, 1865. Not long before the city was abandoned, 1,200 Federal officers, all prisoners of war, were relocated to Charlotte, arriving on February 15. The prison was located "in a pine grove" and called Camp Necessity, Camp Bacon or Camp Exchange. Due to a lack of guards, fifteen prisoners escaped that night, with nine recaptured the next day. Major Elias Griswold was in command. A few days later, orders arrived to transfer the prisoners to Goldsboro, North Carolina, where presumably they were exchanged. Lieutenant Allen Abbott, Nineteenth New York Cavalry, was one of the prisoners. He recalled arriving in Charlotte on the afternoon of February 15 and marching three-quarters of a mile through the mud to the camp, where the prisoners "received the first meat we had had in over one hundred and thirty days." Abbott found "a few old 'A' tents for shelter," but little else. "The ground was soft and warm, and the water we drank was obtained from an old goose-pond." The next day, Colonel Hoke visited the camp, interviewing the prisoners and informing them that the Confederates were planning to parole them. The guard surrounding the prisoners was "totally inefficient and terribly demoralized," and Federal prisoners escaped often. Hoke sent word to the camp, asking the Federals "not to straggle up town, as they had a very strong police guard, and some of them might get into trouble." Some gave the prisoners money to purchase provisions. Soon, the Federal prisoners were gone.[86]

The Federals left Columbia in ruins in February and headed north, toward Charlotte, destroying the tracks of the Charlotte and South Carolina Railroad as they advanced. Most in Charlotte were well acquainted with the atrocities committed by the Federal army of William T. Sherman and feared that the Queen City would suffer the same fate as Atlanta and Columbia. After wrecking the railroad north of Columbia, Sherman's forces turned toward the northeast, choosing instead to strike toward Fayetteville. The Federals were in possession of Wilmington by this time, and Sherman could connect with them for supplies. Remnants of the Confederate Army

Confederate general Joseph Johnson passed through Charlotte on several occasions and even had his headquarters here in 1865. *Library of Congress.*

of Tennessee filed into Charlotte. Confederate general P.G.T. Beauregard recommended on February 17 that Charlotte be abandoned. On February 21, he told Hoke to double the guard in Charlotte to prevent pillaging and to arrest officers and men lacking the proper papers. Beauregard was in

Charlotte on February 22, when he was told that General Joseph Johnston had been assigned as commander of the troops from Tennessee, Georgia, South Carolina and Florida. For a few days, Beauregard and Johnston made their headquarters in Charlotte. Beauregard was serenaded by some of the soldiers while in town, after which Beauregard gave a short speech. On March 1, Johnston wrote that he had six thousand infantry and light artillery with him at Charlotte and recommended that these men be transferred via the railroad to Smithville, in eastern North Carolina. The troops were soon moving, and on March 4, Johnston transferred his headquarters to Fayetteville. Johnston consolidated troops from various commands and pitched into a portion of Sherman's army near Bentonville later that month. Though the Confederates initially beat back large portions of the Federal army, Federal reinforcements made Johnston's position untenable, forcing his retreat.[87]

Bentonville produced 2,600 Confederate casualties. Many were loaded onto trains and shipped back to Raleigh, Greensboro and even Charlotte. A couple of days after the battle, Charlotte citizens formed an Ambulance Committee to assist with the arriving sick and wounded. They elected John Brown chairman, and he encouraged that the people from surrounding counties bring "food—Butter, eggs, Fowls, Dried Fruit, Vegetables, Milk" for those coming in daily. Members of the committee were assigned to meet each train arriving in town. Various buildings about town were converted into makeshift wards to accommodate varying numbers of patients: Elias & Cohen's store (150); Morse's store (100); Red House, opposite the Presbyterian Church (100); Koopmann & Phelps's store (100); Treloar's Hall (100); William and Gray (50); storeroom next to Branch bank (50); and Burrows's store (50). Added to this was the General Hospital, with room for 500. There were also one hundred tents "stretched along the outskirts of… town each containing one or more wounded soldiers." All told, that was enough room for 1,300 men. There was some concern that local churches might be needed. Surgeon Gibbon was in charge of the whole system, with several assistant surgeons supporting him.[88]

The ladies of Charlotte continued to be "angels of mercy" in the hospitals, thronging "the different wards daily [with] good wholesome food and many rich delicacies." The papers continued to list the contributions brought in, including "1 trunk, 2 bags and 1 basket provisions, wines, cakes, &c" by the ladies of Davidson College, among others. On April 11, one of the hospital patients wrote a public letter of appreciation to these ladies, expressing his surprise at how they had "kept up the spirit of

Federal general William T. Sherman feinted north from Columbia, South Carolina, toward Charlotte. *Library of Congress.*

cheering and assisting the wounded, sick and weary soldiers." The ladies obviously made an indelible impression on their charges. One old soldier wrote a letter that appeared in an 1893 newspaper, wanting to identify the visitors. "Two ladies with a negro came to see the sick every day…One was an aged lady, the other a young lady…The negro carried the basket of victuals…I occupied the first bunk on the right of the door as you came in," recalled the old soldier from Georgia.[89]

"Darkness seemed now to close swiftly over the Confederacy," wrote Varina Davis, wife of Confederate president Jefferson Davis. On March 29, the president took her, their children, his sister-in-law Maggie Howell, and two servants, including Jim Limber, a six-year-old black orphan the family had adopted, and put them on a train from Richmond to Charlotte. They were escorted by the president's private secretary, Burton Harrison, and joined by the daughters of secretary of the treasury, George Trenholm, escorted by midshipman James Morgan. "There were no other passengers," wrote Harrison, "and the train consisted of only two or three cars." It took four days for the party to reach Charlotte, where it took considerable effort to find accommodations for Varina and her children. They finally rented a house owned by Abram Weill, a merchant and member of Charlotte's Jewish community. Varina found the morale of people in Charlotte exceedingly low, although the post officers, who paid her a visit with their wives, were "exceedingly kind." In her letter to the president, she mentioned other refugees, such as the wife of General Johnston, who was "living with the cashier of the bank and family"; the family of Raphael Semmes, then in the process of heading farther south; and the family of Confederate senator Louis Wigfall, staying with Mrs. Johnston.[90]

Also boxed up and sent south via the railroad were papers from various Confederate departments and bureaus. Many of these were under the charge of William Bromwell, State Department clerk. The State Department records were deposited in the Mecklenburg courthouse in crates marked with Bromwell's initials. The War Department papers were stored in Charlotte, along with the Treasury Department papers and possibly the Ordnance Department and Navy Department papers. The papers of the Confederate Congress and Post Office Department continued farther south into South Carolina.[91]

Federal soldiers broke through Confederate defenses south of Petersburg on April 2, 1865, and the Confederate government evacuated Richmond that evening. Captain William Parker, superintendent of the Confederate Naval Academy, and his battalion of naval cadets were ordered to take charge of

In April 1865, Federal soldiers from General George Stoneman's command attacked along the Catawba River. *Library of Congress.*

the Confederate treasury that evening and convey it to Danville, Virginia, then to Greensboro and finally on to Charlotte. On April 8, the gold and silver bullion were deposited in the old United States Mint building, along with the papers from the Treasury Department.[92]

Davis himself, along with all but one of his cabinet, also left Richmond, setting up a temporary capital in Danville. With the surrender of the Army of Northern Virginia at Appomattox Court House on April 9, the position at Danville became untenable. Davis and his party moved by train to Greensboro, North Carolina. Fearing capture, Varina Davis and her family, along with the Confederate treasury, headed into South Carolina on April 11.

Charlotte residents had even more reason to agonize. Major General George Stoneman led a division of Federal cavalry into western North Carolina on March 27–28. They proceeded west, through Boone and Wilkesboro, before turning north and into Virginia on April 2. They returned to North Carolina April 9, moving through Germantown and striking the railroad around Greensboro. When President Davis and his party moved from Greensboro to Charlotte on April 15, they were forced to abandon the train and travel on horseback or in ambulances. Stoneman fought a battle on the outskirts of Salisbury on April 12, capturing the town and burning an immense quality of military equipment. After being defeated in an attempt to capture the bridge over the Yadkin River, Stoneman turned his attention back west. On Easter Sunday (April 16), Stoneman dispatched a brigade of cavalry to "scout down the Catawba River towards Charlotte."[93]

Mecklenburg County and Charlotte were abuzz with activity on the impending arrival of Stoneman's raiders. The Confederate State Department papers at the courthouse were moved out of town. Gold and silver from the vaults of the North Carolina Bank branch in Charlotte was loaded into a wagon under the cover of darkness and taken to a farm and buried. The county records were also "sent off to the country" by officials. Charlotte residents John Young and William Myers formed a home guard company, made up of men exempt from regular service. The men were mustered in for three months. A group of ladies penned a letter to post commander William Hoke on April 19, decrying the lack of male protection. They asked Hoke to appoint a day and time when they could be armed and trained to defend themselves and their loved ones.[94]

Federal forces took Nation's Ford on the Catawba River April 19, capturing the Confederate pickets guarding the area and burning the bridge. Confederate cavalry soon arrived to skirmish with the Federals across the river, trading shots for a couple hours. At the same time, another detachment of the Twelfth Ohio Cavalry rode toward Tuckaseegee Ford, destroying the gunpowder mill and part of the Confederate Acid Works. Once again, Confederate cavalry attacked, but was held in place by the Federals. Beatties Ford and Cowan's Ford were also captured, while skirmishing took place at the Wilmington, Charlotte and Rutherford Railroad bridge over the Catawba River, which was burned. At Rozzell's Ferry, a defensive line was formed by Brigadier General Robert Johnston and a handful of Confederates. Johnston had been at home on a furlough for wounds when he learned of the Federal advance toward Charlotte. The Federals appeared on a hill overlooking the river and opened fire. "I stated to the officer with me that I thought we had best retire," wrote Johnston after the war; then, "a bullet struck me on my left side, just over my heart. The shock was so severe that it sickened me, and I fell on my horse's neck, thinking it had passed through my body." Johnston was lucky: the round had struck a half-dollar in his breast pocket, saving his life. Confederate forces retreated, and the Federals burned the bridge. The squads and detachments that captured the various bridges and fords to the west of Charlotte advanced no further. They lacked the numbers to contend with the Confederate forces in the Queen City.[95]

Following a several days' overland journey, President Davis and his cabinet arrived in Charlotte on April 19. According to Burton Harrison, only one citizen was willing to entertain Davis. Everyone else feared having the house burned by the Federals. Davis's host was Lewis Bates, the Northern-born telegraph company agent. He was a bachelor, with only one servant, who kept a "sort of 'open house,'" where a broad, well equipped sideboard was the most conspicuous—not at all a seemly place for Mr. Davis." Yet Davis had no other option. William Johnston greeted the president at the Bates home. Confederate cavalry came down the street, "waving their flags and hurrahed for 'Jefferson Davis.'" Davis was in the process of delivering a speech "when he was interrupted by J.C. Courtney, manager of the telegraph office, who handed him a telegraph, which he opened, read and handed to William Johnston, who was standing by his side. There were cries from the crowd 'Read!' 'Read!' whereupon Colonel Johnston read the telegram… announcing…that Mr. Lincoln had been assassinated." Davis was stunned with disbelief at the news, as were others in Charlotte. One Confederate soldier passing through noted in his journal that "there is a startling rumor afloat that President Abe Lincoln has been killed." It is unclear just how widespread this information was.[96]

This bronze plaque on South Tryon Street indicates the spot where Jefferson Davis learned of the death of Abraham Lincoln. *Public Library of Charlotte-Mecklenburg County.*

The last meeting of the entire Confederate cabinet took place at the home of William Phifer on North Tryon Street. *University of North Carolina-Charlotte.*

Davis and some of his staff officers stayed with Bates; Harrison and Secretary of State Judah Benjamin with Abram Weill; Attorney General George Davis boarded with William Myers; Secretary of War John Breckenridge with Joe Hilburn; Secretary of the Treasury George Trenholm at the Phifers's; Stephen Mallory, Secretary of the Navy, at the Taylor residence; and, John Reagan, Secretary of the Post Office, possibly also at the Taylor home.[97]

"We hear rumors of an armistice, and that flags of truce have been flying around in all directions," confided Curtis Burke in his journal. Burke was a paroled Confederate prisoner of war, and like so many others, was passing through the Queen City. Over the next few days, messages passed between the Confederate army under Joseph Johnston at Greensboro, Federal commander William Sherman in Raleigh and Davis in Charlotte. Johnston wanted to surrender not only his army, but civil officials like Davis as well. Davis agreed, and Sherman sent the proposal to his superiors in Washington. They refused, saying Sherman had overstepped his authority. New negotiations were conducted between Johnston and Sherman. On April 26, Johnston surrendered his army at the Bennett Place outside Durham. Johnston returned to Charlotte to meet with Davis. Governor Vance followed, and Davis believed that Vance was joining him for a last stand. Davis wanted to move beyond the Mississippi River, joining Confederates there and recruiting a new army. For this purpose, he hoped Vance would join him with as many North Carolina soldiers as possible. General Breckenridge intervened, saying that possibilities were too remote and that Vance should stay and take care of the people in North Carolina. Davis agreed, and as Vance left, added, "God bless you, sir, and the noble old State of North Carolina."[98]

For a week, Charlotte was the capital of the Confederate government. Unlike Danville or Greensboro, in Charlotte, all of the cabinet was present for a time, although Breckenridge was kept busy between Charlotte and Greensboro. The cabinet met in the director's room at the branch office of the North Carolina Bank, and due to the illness of Trenholm, at William Phifer's home, where the last official meeting of the entire cabinet took place on April 26, 1865. Davis wrote letters and dispatches, and other cabinet members and officers attempted to carry out their responsibilities. General Josiah Gorgas recalled examining a cadet for promotion with other officers "in the...upper story of a warehouse in Charlotte."[99]

With Johnston unable to surrender the civil officials, Davis had no choice but to flee south. It was at Charlotte that the Confederate government fractured. Some members, like George Davis and Samuel Cooper, declined to go farther. Davis left on April 26 and was captured on May 10 in Georgia.

There were thousands of Confederate soldiers milling about Charlotte, just waiting. On April 29, Major General Joseph Wheeler penned his farewell address to his cavalry corps. "Gallant Comrades—You have fought your last fight, your task is done," Wheeler wrote. He commended them on the battles they had fought and lamented the comrades slain and left on the fields. "You have done all that human exertion could accomplish…Brethren in the cause of freedom, comrades in arms, I bid you farewell," Wheeler concluded.[100]

Charlotte was spared the destruction inflicted on places like Atlanta, Columbia and Richmond. Much of the infrastructure remained intact. The rails to the north and south were wrecked, but the line to Greensboro was repaired within days. The greatest toll that Charlotte and Mecklenburg County paid was in lives. John B. Alexander estimated that 2,713 men served in the Confederate army, a low estimate not including the junior or senior reserves or the three companies of detailed men. At least 638 of them died during the war, killed on a battlefield or dying of disease, somewhere around 23 percent.

There was one final piece of the wartime drama. Over six thousand slaves in Mecklenburg County gained their freedom at the end of the war. Some had probably already heard of their impending emancipation before the end of the fighting. On the day that William Paterson learned that the Confederacy had collapsed, he went to the fields where his slaves were working and told them they were free, but asked them to stay on and work to the end of the year. Seven of them agreed to be paid for their labors, either with provisions or money. It was a start on a very long road toward a new South and a new Charlotte.[101]

Chapter 7

Soldiers of the Gray and Blue

*"He Could Not Die More Nobly or in
a More Noble Cause"*

Writing about the exploits of the nearly three thousand Mecklenburg men who fought in the Confederate armies would take several volumes. There are, however, a few individuals whose memorable stories illustrate the range of these experiences.

RUFUS BARRINGER

Rufus Clay Barringer was not a typical fire-breathing secessionist. Politically, he was opposed to secession and advocated Negro suffrage. The Cabarrus County native was born in December 1821, graduating from the University of North Carolina in 1842, before practicing law in Concord. In 1854, Barringer married Eugenia Morrison, becoming a brother-in-law to Daniel Hill and Thomas "Stonewall" Jackson. Even though he opposed secession, he felt, like many others, compelled to defend North Carolina, and he enlisted in the Cabarrus Rangers, which became Company F, First North Carolina Cavalry. Barringer was elected captain, and in August 1863, he was promoted to major of the regiment. Two months later, he was promoted to lieutenant colonel, later serving as commander of the Fourth North Carolina Cavalry. Eugenia died before the war, and Barringer married Rosalie Chunn of Charlotte during the war. Barringer fought in seventy-six engagements and was wounded three times. Commissioned brigadier general in June 1864,

Barringer was captured at Namozine Church, Virginia, on April 3, 1865. While at City Point Prison, Barringer met Abraham Lincoln, the president's first meeting with a Confederate general. Charlotte became Barringer's home after the war, where he practiced law, became a Republican and served in the 1875 Constitutional Convention. He ran for lieutenant governor in 1880, but lost. General Barringer died on February 3, 1896, and he is buried at Elmwood Cemetery in Charlotte.[102]

DANIEL HARVEY HILL

Born in York District, South Carolina, in July 1821, Daniel Hill was the grandson of two Revolutionary War soldiers. A West Point graduate, Hill earned two brevet promotions for gallantry in combat during the Mexican War, and the state of South Carolina later presented him with a sword. In 1849, Hill resigned from the army and began teaching mathematics at Washington College in Lexington, Virginia. Hill married Isabella Morrison, daughter of the first president of Davidson College, and was brother-in-law to both Thomas "Stonewall" Jackson and Rufus Barringer. Two years later, Hill joined the faculty of Davidson College, soon occupying the chair of the mathematics department. When the North Carolina Military Institute was created, Hill resigned from Davidson College to become superintendent in 1859.

North Carolina governor John Ellis asked Hill to establish a training camp in Raleigh in April 1861, promoting Hill to the rank of colonel at the same time. Soon, Hill assumed command of the First North Carolina Volunteers, leading the regiment into Virginia and into battle at Big Bethel Church, southeast of Richmond. Hill was promoted to brigadier general in September 1861 and major general in March 1862. During the battles of Seven Days, South Mountain and Sharpsburg, Hill's division served conspicuously. After a stint in the defenses around Richmond and in eastern North Carolina, Hill was transferred to the Army of Tennessee, where he held corps command. On July 11, 1863, Hill was nominated as lieutenant general, but he was not confirmed by the Confederate senate. From October 1863 until May 1864, Hill was back in Charlotte: Hill had criticized Army of Tennessee commander Braxton Bragg one too many times, and Jefferson Davis had relieved him of command. Hill later served on the staff of P.G.T. Beauregard and held other commands before rejoining the Army of Tennessee in time to fight at the battle of Bentonville, North Carolina, in March 1865. At Greensboro, May 1, 1865, Hill received his parole and returned to Charlotte. Historian John Barrett once wrote that "There was no greater waste of general-officer material during the war than...Hill, one of the best combat soldiers... in the Confederate army. Unfortunately, he suffered from an incontrollable impulse to criticize his associates."

Following the war, Hill published *The Land We Love* and, in 1869, a weekly newspaper, *The Southern Home*. From 1877 to 1884, Hill served as president of the Arkansas Industrial University (present-day University of Arkansas) and, from 1885 to 1889, the Middle Georgia Military and Agricultural College. Hill died in Charlotte on September 24, 1889, and he is buried at the Davidson College Cemetery.[103]

Daniel Harvey Hill was superintendent of the North Carolina Military institute. He rose to the rank of major general and lived in Charlotte after the war. *Library of Congress.*

CHARLES LEE

"A Brave Man Fallen," read the headlines of the *Western Democrat*, in reference to Charles Cochrane Lee. Born on February 2, 1834, in Charleston, South Carolina, Lee grew up in Asheville, where his father ran a boys' school. In 1852, Lee entered West Point, graduating fourth in his class four years later, the same year that he married Anna Tripp. Lee resigned from the

Thirty-seventh North Carolina Troops Flag. Over four hundred Mecklenburg County men served under the flag of the Thirty-seventh NCT, led by Colonel Charles C. Lee. *Museum of the Confederacy.*

army in 1859 and took a position at the North Carolina Military Institute in Charlotte, teaching chemistry, mineralogy, geology and infantry tactics, along with being the commander of cadets. In 1861, Lee was appointed by Governor Ellis to purchase North Carolina's war munitions. Lee's task took him into the Northern states. However, he was back in the South in time to serve in the ordnance department in South Carolina under Beauregard in April 1861. On May 11, Lee was elected lieutenant colonel of the First North Carolina Volunteers, fighting at Big Bethel, Virginia, the next month. On the advance of Hill to brigadier general, Lee was promoted to colonel of the Bethel Regiment. After this regiment was mustered out of service, Lee was elected colonel on November 20, 1861, of the Thirty-seventh North Carolina Troops.

Lee, in command of a demi-brigade, fought at New Bern, North Carolina, before being transferred to Virginia as a part of a North Carolina brigade commanded by Lawrence O'Bryan Branch. Colonel Lee led his regiment through the battles of Hanover Court House and Mechanicsville. On June 30, 1862, at the battle of Frayser's Farm, while Lee led the Thirty-seventh North Carolina against a battery of Federal artillery, he encouraged his men with "On, my brave boys!" and was struck and killed by cannon fire. When told of his death, his soldiers "wept as if they had lost a father." Lee's remains were taken back to Charlotte where he was interred on July 3, 1862, in Elmwood Cemetery. The *North Carolina Whig* reported on July 8: "Thus died upon the altar of his country one of nature's noblemen. None knew him but to love him, a gentleman, a scholar, a true soldier fallen. May his memory ever remain fresh in our hearts, his monument a nation's gratitude. Peace to his ashes." Colonel Lee was survived by his wife and their four children.[104]

EGBERT ROSS

While most men between the ages of eighteen and fifty served in the Confederate army, in many ways, the Civil War was a young man's war. Egbert A. Ross was one of those young men. Born in 1842, Ross attended both the North Carolina Military Institute and the Hillsboro Military Institute prior to the war. He enlisted in a local militia group and, on April 25, became captain of the "Charlotte Grays." The company was reorganized in February 1862, joining the Eleventh North Carolina State Troops. Ross, at the age of nineteen, became major of the regiment in May 1862. For much of 1862 and early 1863, the regiment was

Egbert Ross, pictured here as captain of the Charlotte Grays, was killed at Gettysburg on July 1, 1863. *Major Egbert A. Ross Camp, Sons of Confederate Veterans.*

on garrison duty in southeastern Virginia and eastern North Carolina. In January 1863, the regiment was assigned to James Pettigrew's brigade, and then transferred to Virginia in May 1863, assigned to Henry Heth's division. On July 1, Pettigrew's brigade attacked the Federals positioned along McPherson's Ridge, just to the west of Gettysburg, Pennsylvania, in "one of the bloodiest actions of the Civil War"; Ross was killed in action and his cousin Daniel Hill later wrote to Ross's mother, "I hope that you can look more calmly at the event as being ordered by a wise and merciful God. Young as your brave boy was, he had done much service; he had won the confidence of his regiment and the country, and has left a name behind of which any father might justly be proud. I am sure you would rather have him as your dead Egbert than to have him saved by ingloriously keeping out of service, he had to die at some time, and surely he could not die more nobly or in a more noble cause." Ross's remains were later interred in Elmwood Cemetery in Charlotte.[105]

MECKLENBURG COUNTY CITIZENS AT THE FAMOUS BATTLE BETWEEN THE *MONITOR* AND *MERRIMACK*

The famous duel between the USS *Monitor* and the CSS *Virginia* is a well-known story. When the Federal forces abandoned the naval yard in Norfolk, Virginia, the USS *Merrimac*, a wooden frigate in dock for repairs, was sunk and burned. However, Confederate forces were able to salvage much of the hull and, more importantly, the engines. Soon, work began on a new type of warship with iron plating able to deflect cannon shot. The *Merrimac* was soon rechristened the CSS *Virginia*. She needed a crew, and naval officers started scouring nearby infantry regiments. Many actual sailors came from a Louisiana regiment, but others came from Virginia, Georgia and South Carolina regiments, and twenty-two men left the Thirteenth and Fourteenth North Carolina State Troops, both stationed near Yorktown, Virginia. Five of those from the Thirteenth Regiment had connections with Mecklenburg County. Two, Henry Johnston and Seth Hotckiss, were farmers from South Carolina who had enlisted in Mecklenburg. John Baker was a twenty-two-year-old farmer from Mecklenburg; James (or Josiah) Davis was a twenty-four-year-old Mecklenburg County farmer; and James Sheffield, a Virginia native, worked in the tobacco industry in Charlotte. All five transferred to the crew of the *Virginia* in February 1862 and were listed as landsmen, the

Several men from Mecklenburg County served on the CSS *Virginia* during its famous duel with the USS *Monitor* in 1862. *Harper's Weekly.*

lowest rank in the Confederate navy. The great duel between the *Monitor* and the *Virginia* was fought March 9, 1862, in the waters at Hampton Roads, Virginia, the day after the *Virginia* had destroyed or damaged several wooden Union warships. Neither the *Monitor* nor the *Virginia* made much headway in the duel. That evening, the *Virginia* sailed back to port for repairs. There would be much posturing for the next two months, but neither ship again engaged the other. When the Confederates abandoned the Peninsula below Richmond in May 1862, the Virginia was unable to sail up the James River and was burned by the Confederates. The crew was transferred. Interestingly, the *Monitor* sank off the coast of North Carolina on December 31, 1862. Tracing the North Carolina crewmembers of the *Virginia* is a challenge, as Confederate Naval records are incomplete. Many of the crew served on the CSS *Chattahoochee* on the Apalachicola River in Florida. At least one, Sheffield, survived the war.

THE GIBBON BROTHERS

Often, the Civil War is referred to as a war in which brother fought against brother. While Charlotte and Mecklenburg County were decidedly pro-Confederate, cases of brother-versus-brother can still be found. No case is a better example than that of the Gibbon brothers of Charlotte. Dr. John Gibbon, Charlotte's first assayer at the United States Mint, had several sons, including Robert who attended local Mecklenburg County schools, then Yale University and the Jefferson Medical College in Philadelphia. In 1848, he

John Gibbon grew up in Charlotte and later attended West Point. Unlike his brothers Nicholas and Robert, John fought for the Union, attaining the rank of major general. *Library of Congress.*

returned to Charlotte and began practicing medicine until enlisting in the Twenty-eighth North Carolina Troops; he was appointed surgeon on September 25, 1861. Robert served in this regiment until appointed surgeon of James Lane's North Carolina brigade in January 1864. Later that year, he was appointed surgeon of the Charlotte hospitals. Robert continued practicing in Charlotte until his 1898 death when he was laid to rest in Elmwood Cemetery. His brother Nicholas Gibbon was born in 1837 and also attended Jefferson Medical College. Nicholas enlisted in the First North Carolina Volunteers, fighting at Big Bethel in June 1861. He later served as assistant commissary of substance in the Twenty-eighth North Carolina Troops and eventually became a division-level staff officer under Cadmus Wilcox. After the war, he farmed and served in the General Assembly before he died in October 1917 and was buried at Sugar Creek Presbyterian Church. A third brother, John Gibbon, was born in 1827 and graduated from West Point in 1847. John then served in Mexico, Florida and Texas and taught artillery tactics at West Point. When the war commenced, John served in the artillery before being promoted to brigadier general of volunteers in May 1862. He was considered "one of the Army of the Potomac's premier combat leaders." John commanded the Iron Brigade at Gettysburg. In June 1864, he was promoted to the rank of major general and received command of the XXIV Corps, Army of the James. Gibbon was one of the commissioners in charge of paroling the remaining members of the Confederate Army of Northern

Virginia at Appomattox in 1865. Following the war, he continued to serve in the Regular army, until his retirement in 1885. He died in 1896 and is buried at Arlington National Cemetery.

During the war, in the fall of 1864, John Gibbon wrote his brother Nicholas, proposing that the two meet between the lines, a mini-family reunion. John had permission from his commanding officer, Lieutenant General U.S. Grant. Nicholas declined John's invitation: "It is not agreeable that I should meet you under the circumstances proposed in your note, although I have no doubt that I could obtain permission from General Lee if I desired."[106]

WILLIAM OWENS

Few exhibited as much patriotism as Charlotte mayor William A. Owens. The twenty-seven-year-old Owens, a graduate of the University of North Carolina, enlisted on April 16, 1861, more than a month before North Carolina left the Union, in the Hornet's Nest Riflemen. The governor appointed Owens a first lieutenant in what became Company B, First North Carolina Volunteers, on May 13, 1861. Owens was soon in Virginia, fighting at the battle of Big Bethel in June. When the captain of Company B, William Lewis, resigned to take a government job, Owens was promoted to captain. His regiment was mustered out of service in November 1861, and Owens returned to Charlotte, where he was elected mayor in January 1862. A couple weeks passed, and he was appointed major of the Thirty-fourth North Carolina Troops. Three months later, Owens was elected lieutenant colonel of the Eleventh North Carolina State Troops and transferred. In May 1862, he was promoted to colonel and took command of the Fifty-third North Carolina Troops. Owens was wounded during the Battle of Spotsylvania Court House on May 12, 1864. On July 18, 1864, Colonel Owens had just returned from convalescent leave, when his regiment was called onto the field. A portion of the Confederate army, under General Jubal Early, had advanced through the Shenandoah Valley and attacked the outer perimeter of Washington, D.C. The attack was an effort to draw Federal troops away from the embattled defenses of Richmond and Petersburg, Virginia. As Early's forces fell back, they were pursued by Federal troops. These Federal soldiers attempted to push their way through Snicker's Gap and the Shenandoah Valley, but were met and crushed by Confederate forces. Colonel Owens was wounded in the bowels on July 18, just two hours after returning to camp. He died the next day. Owens was originally interred at the Old Stone Church in Berryville, Virginia, and was later reburied in the Old Settlers Cemetery in Charlotte.[107]

THE IMMORTAL SIX HUNDRED

War produces many heartrending accounts. One of the saddest of these concerns the fates of the men captured in battle. Thousands of soldiers, both blue and gray, perished in prison camps. Even more tragic are the fates of six hundred Confederate soldiers, almost all officers, used as human shields in late 1864 by the Federal army outside Charleston, South Carolina. In early 1864, six hundred Federal officers were moved from the prison camp in Macon, Georgia, to Charleston, South Carolina. These men were on their way to other prison facilities. Unfortunately for the Federal officers, the civilian sections of Charleston were frequently bombarded by Federal cannons from Sullivan's Island and other Federal batteries in the area. While there is no documentation that Union officers were intentionally put in harm's way, the Federal commander in the area quickly retaliated by placing six hundred Confederate officers in front of the battery on Morris Island. On August 13, these men were drawn from the Fort Delaware Prison Camp and sent south. Two Mecklenburg County men, Lieutenant Alexander Cathey and Private William Johnson, were among those called. Cathey, a member of the Thirty-fourth North Carolina Troops, was captured after being wounded at Gettysburg, losing a leg in the process. Johnson was a member of the First North Carolina Cavalry captured at Bristoe Station, Virginia, November 1863. After eighteen days in the cargo hold of a ship, the men disembarked on September 7. The prisoners were placed under the guard of the Fifty-fourth Massachusetts Infantry. The third great bombardment of Charleston began the next day, with the Confederates in a stockade in front of the heavy Federal siege cannons. For fifty days, they remained there, none ever struck by incoming Confederate fire. On October 21, the Confederates were shipped to Fort Pulaski, near Savannah, Georgia. They remained at Fort Pulaski until March 4, 1865, surviving on cornmeal and pickles, supplemented by caught rats and cats. Cathey, probably due to the loss of his leg, was paroled in Charleston on December 15, 1864, while Johnson was not released from prison until June 1865.[108]

Chapter 8

Reconstruction: "We Are Tired of Turmoil and Disputes, and Want to Do All in Our Power to Promote Peace"

For the Southern soldiers, the war ended in April 1865 when Lee surrendered at Appomattox and Johnston surrendered at the Bennett Place. Soldiers received their paroles and began the arduous trip home. In Charlotte, the war was entering a new phase. On May 7, a company of the Ninth New Jersey Infantry arrived. Captain Morris Runyon found Charlotte full of Confederates: some from the armies of Lee and Johnston and others who had not yet been surrendered and paroled. Raids, drunkenness and disorder were rampant. Moving through the northern part of Mecklenburg County, the Federal soldiers encountered thousands of former Confederates and "also citizens—stragglers, who were out to steal cotton, clothing, provisions—in short, anything they could lay their hands on." Bank president James Carson wrote long after the war: "[For] some two or three weeks there was much disorder and lawlessness about Charlotte. Bands of Confederate Cavalry were the worst. They would seize a man's horse or mule in the main streets and carry them off." Runyon assumed command, issuing orders and "prohibiting the sale of all kinds of spirituous liquors."[109]

Runyon made a tour of the town, finding hordes of former Confederate soldiers and refugees, as well as numerous items once shipped to Charlotte for safekeeping. George Peters of the Ninth New Jersey reported that the abandoned medical purveyor's office contained "great quantities of medicines…such as morphine and nitre…all with English labels…which had been procured by blockade-running." Also captured were four cannon, "about 900 small arms; 400,000 percussion-caps; 1,400 pounds of powder;

[and] an immense quantity of sabres, cutlasses, etc., cartridge-boxes, and other equipments."[110]

Undoubtedly the most important of Runyon's finds was over eighty crates belonging to the Confederate War Department. Samuel Cooper, Adjutant and Inspector General and the highest-ranking Confederate officer, had remained in Charlotte with the records when Davis departed. Cooper informed Joseph Johnston of the location of the papers, and on May 8, Johnston telegraphed General Schofield that information. Johnston believed the papers could "furnish valuable materials for history." Schofield dispatched Lieutenant G.P. Washburne to retrieve them. When Washburne came calling on the evening of May 14, Johnston was out, but replied to Washburne's note that the documents had already been turned over to the local post commander. However, Johnston agreed to meet with Washburne the next morning. An observer noted that the papers were stored in a building on an unnamed main street, "in a cellar—a dark, dismal spot...wagons were procured, and the boxes containing the documents conveyed to the railroad" and then taken to Raleigh. There were eighty-three boxes "of various sizes, from an ammunition box to a large clothing chest...They were also of all shapes. Some of them are rifle boxes, and many of them resemble the ordinary army mess chest." These papers were transported via ship to Washington, D.C.[111]

In Charlotte, Captain Runyon found the citizens "very hospitable; the rich and well-to-do class seemed to be very well satisfied with the change; the middle-class and the poor spoke bitterly and with condemnation of Jefferson Davis and his clique." Company G was released from duties and returned to Greensboro.[112]

Orders came on May 10 for the First Division, XXIII Corps to depart from Greensboro and head to Charlotte. Under the command of Brigadier General Thomas Ruger, the First Division contained several thousand men. Ruger arrived in Charlotte on May 14, establishing his headquarters in the mint building, while the division hospital took over the buildings of the military institute. Federal soldiers camped all over the city. Later in July, a review of Federal soldiers was held, with four thousand men marching through the streets. By May 30, Colonel William Warner, commander of the 180th Ohio Volunteer Infantry, was considered the post commander in Charlotte.[113]

One of the first orders of business for the Federals was issuing paroles for thousands of Confederate soldiers in Charlotte. It is unclear if Ruger brought pre-printed forms or used a local press. Some of the soldiers were from North Carolina regiments, possibly sick in one of the hospitals or maybe stragglers or deserters. Thomas Alexander of the Fifty-eighth North

Carolina Troops was wounded near Atlanta on August 5, 1864. The crippled Alexander was in Charlotte where he took the oath and was paroled May 11, 1865. Hundreds of cavalrymen, members of the lamented John H. Morgan's command, roamed the streets. Four Confederate generals also received their paroles: Samuel Cooper, William Allen, Robert Johnson and Evander Law. There were 4,015 former Confederates who received their paroles in the Queen City. These paroles were simple pieces of papers stating that the soldiers would not take up arms until properly paroled, while obeying the laws where they lived.[114]

Federal major general John Schofield, upon taking control of the state, declared the war over in North Carolina in April 1865. *Library of Congress.*

Union general John Schofield assumed command of North Carolina in April 1865. On April 27, he issued an order declaring the war over in the Tar Heel state. For the next month, North Carolina was without civilian leadership. Governor Vance was arrested at his home in Statesville on May 13, 1865, and spent the next couple of months in prison in Washington, D.C. On May 29, Vice President Andrew Johnson, who assumed the presidency on the death of Lincoln, issued two proclamations regarding his Reconstruction policy. The first granted general amnesty to all former Confederates except to those who fell into one of fourteen classes. These classes included those who held the rank of colonel or above; who worked for the Confederate government; or whose property was valued at $20,000 or more. Those who fell into one of these classes had to apply to the president (through the governor) for a presidential pardon. In Charlotte and Mecklenburg County, thirty-nine citizens filed for a presidential pardon. Former major general Daniel Hill applied for his pardon in July 1865, stating that he had never maltreated Federal soldiers

Andrew Johnson became president of the United States following the death of Abraham Lincoln. *Library of Congress.*

or citizens of the United States. His pardon sat unanswered until June 1867. Twelve of the applicants were former postmasters. Elam King, postmaster at Morrison's Tan Yard, stated "he was post master previous to the breaking out of the rebellion and was forced by the Confederate Government to receive a new appointment." Had King not accepted this position, the post office would likely have been closed. M.W. Alexander was a mail agent on the Charlotte and South Carolina Railroad. He stated in his application that he had a large family to support and that was his sole reason for accepting a Confederate position. Being the mail agent also kept him out of the Confederate army. An interesting and unique petition was that of Mrs. Margaret Withers. Of the approximately 15,000 applications for presidential pardon, only 389 were from women, including 21 from North Carolina. Withers stated that in 1860, the family's property was valued at more than $20,000. Her husband, Samuel, had enlisted in 1863 and died in 1864, leaving behind four small children. She was asking Johnson for a "special pardon with restoration of rights of property in behalf of herself and infant children." There was much talk at this time on the redistribution of Confederate lands to former slaves. Withers was thus concerned that she and her children would be left destitute.[115]

Johnson's second proclamation on May 29 dealt directly with North Carolina: he named William Holden as provisional governor. Holden, who was despised across the state for his role in the peace movement, faced a monumental task: restoring Federal laws, taxes and customs collections. This included filling all leadership positions with loyal men. Furthermore, Holden was charged with the election of delegates and the calling of a convention to amend the state constitution.

The *Western Democrat* announced on June 6 that a new police force was organized by the post commander in Charlotte. It was charged with preserving order and quiet "and to prevent injustice and suffering." The entire police force was under the control of the provost marshall, and upon accepting their positions, members had to report to Federal headquarters at the mint to take "the oath of allegiance and also an oath to prevent crime, arrest criminals, and to obey all lawful military orders." R.W. White was appointed captain of the police force, with S.L. Riddle as sergeant and H.M. Phelps as corporal of the Charlotte precinct. Other deputies included Allen Cruse, James Burrows, Leonard Smith and Henry Tate. Appointed magistrates were Thomas Dewey, Charles Overman and F.M. Ross.[116]

Holden appointed Henry Pritchard mayor of Charlotte on June 23, 1865, along with eight aldermen. Pritchard had lived in Charlotte for many years and, in 1858, represented the area in the General Assembly. Commissioners for Charlotte appointed by Holden were W.A. Williams, William Windle, J.E. Stenhouse, A. Weil, J.C. Burroughs, H.M. Phelps, David Barnhardt and C. Hilker.[117]

Post Commander Warner published a variety of orders. Local citizens were encouraged to sell vegetables, fruit, poultry and eggs to Federal soldiers at fair prices, but were forbidden to give or sell liquor. Anyone planning to travel outside town via the railroad had to procure a pass. Citizens were instructed "to thoroughly police their premises," and garbage pickup was scheduled for each Saturday morning. Businesses were closed on Sundays and by 7:00 p.m. each evening.[118]

New businesses slowly began to advertise in the pages of local newspapers. Robert Gibbon, who finished the war as chief surgeon in Charlotte, advertised his surgical services and established an office in the Charlotte Bank building. John Vogel made men's clothing in a shop next to Brown and Stitt's store. J.B. Butler advertised his services in repairing watches, clothes and jewelry. By the end of July, the list of advertisers had grown to at least four columns of newsprint. During the early days of Reconstruction, John Wilkes met with likeminded citizens concerning the formation of a new bank. Wilkes ventured to Washington, D.C., speaking to Freeman Clarke, Comptroller of the Currency, about the process. This information allowed Wilkes to put together a meeting on July 20, 1865, in Charlotte, organizing the first board of directors. On September 11, with Wilkes as president, the First National Bank opened for business.[119]

Despite the positive growth, problems arose between the different factions in Charlotte. On July 25, 1865, the *Western Democrat* published an order demanding that all forms of Confederate rank be removed from jackets, including buttons, rank and braid. "The order was to humiliate the Confederate soldier, and if possible to make 'treason odious,'" wrote John Alexander forty years later. "Nothing was more common…than to see a Yankee cut the buttons from the coat of an ex-Confederate, and immediately see the Federal soldier knocked down."[120]

Alexander's writing, though sometimes seen as divisive, provides a glimpse into postwar conflicts between Federal soldiers and ex-Confederates absent from other sources. Frederick DeWolfe, a former Confederate officer, was plagued by thieves attacking his garden. He requested a guard from the provost and discovered soon thereafter the guard conversing with the thieves "as hail fellows well met." DeWolfe "remonstrated with them, and they cursed him." He then opened fire, killing one of the Federal soldiers. DeWolfe was tried and acquitted, going on to serve as Charlotte's mayor in the 1880s. The horse of Joseph Orr, a former member of the Thirty-seventh North Carolina, was stolen from town one morning. Orr tracked the horse thief back to a saloon full of Federal soldiers, one of whom attacked Orr; the one-armed Confederate knocked him senseless with a hickory stick. Orr was arrested, but escaped back home, where he "loaded his double-barreled shot gun with buckshot and waited in the front porch all night." In another case, John Henderson, a freedman living in the Beatties Ford area, was robbed by Federal soldiers. Henderson went before the post command for justice and the return of the stolen goods. The commander told Henderson that he "could not afford to have his soldiers arrested for petty larceny" and that the Federal commander had "a heap of bad men, and you had better slip off home and say no more about it, for they may do you great harm, maybe kill you." The *Western Democrat* did carry a few stories about conflicts with recently freed slaves. In one issue, the editor lamented that the county jail was full "of these rascals" who "were too lazy to work and of course went to steeling [*sic*]." The editor wanted to know why "some plan [cannot] be adopted to impose punishment upon rogues without keeping them in jail and running the county expense?"[121]

Into this morass stepped the Freedmen's Bureau, created by Congress in March 1865 with the task of helping those displaced and impoverished by the war, to protect former slaves from injustice, to encourage education and to help freedmen find employment and receive fair wages. It was not until June 1865 that a bureau agent, Colonel Eliphalet Whittlesey, was assigned to North Carolina. Whittlesey divided the state into four districts, with assistant superintendents in charge. On June 1, General Ruger assigned Captain John Barnett, 128th Indiana Infantry, to Charlotte. Barnett found "the whole population of Blacks were completely wild." Many of the freedmen had left their homes and were roaming the countryside. That is not to say that all former slaves departed. There are references to the slaves belonging to the Phifer and McCoy families remaining after the war.[122]

Barnett struggled with the large numbers of freedmen. He encouraged them to return to their homes and contract with their former owners, many of whom were struggling themselves. After planting season ended, there simply was not enough work to keep idle hands busy until the fall harvest. Some freedmen did find work. In the Petterson family papers are receipts indicating Ned Petterson was paid five dollars for his time in December 1865. The following December, he was paid twelve bushels of corn, five gallons of molasses and a quantity of cotton. There was also the problem of refugee freedmen, those who had been brought to the Charlotte area from coastal communities as the war progressed and now wanted to return to their homes. In July 1865, Barnett had to deal with fifteen to twenty new refugees who arrived in Charlotte every day, trying to reach their destinations, but with no transportation authorized beyond the state's borders. Later that month, Barnett planned a hospital, school and camp for the destitute. By the end of July, the camp contained fifteen cabins for invalids, aged freemen, women and children who had no other support. Barnett reported that he had 195 freedmen in the camp and another 500 to 600 needing transportation elsewhere. A crude hospital was organized, probably in August, but in October 1865, the bureau assigned Dr. D.H. Abbott to Charlotte and authorized a twenty-five-bed hospital, which was established in January 1866. Barnett's planned school never came to fruition and was left to others. Eventually, Barnett was able to utilize the buildings of the former North Carolina Military Institute. In May 1866, there were 162 refugees living there.[123]

Of course, there were conflicts between the Freedmen's Bureau, freedmen themselves and the former Confederates. In July 1865, Barnett wrote to Whittlesey: "I am not without individual proof of the fact that a great portion of the citizens in my district are taking any and every opportunity to thwart the Government in all of its efforts to establish freedmen in their rights." One former Confederate from Mecklenburg wrote many years after the war: "In almost every instance the Agent appointed to attend to the Freedmen's Bureau was a dishonest character, and of course irritated our people…Any trumped charge by a negro was sufficient to have our best men…in the county appear in person before the Agent, whether charges were true or false, convenient or inconvenient." That is not to say that the Freedmen's Bureau agent was the standard-bearer for the Abolitionist movement. To counter speculations that the farm lands of former Confederates were to be confiscated and divided among the freedmen (the proverbial forty acres and a mule) by December, Barnett issued a circular in October 1865, stating that the rumor was false, adding that "Many of you have become imprudent, lazy, and disrespectful to those which you must look to for your support… Many of you are idling and loafing away their time…while their families are suffering…You alone are accountable for the sad fate that awaits you." Barnett was mustered out of service on April 10, 1866.[124]

There were a few others who were also trying to help the freedmen. E.H. Hill, a missionary with the African Methodist Episcopal Zion Church, reached Charlotte in May 1865, helping to organize Clinton Chapel. The Reverends Sidney Murkland, Willis Miller and Samuel Alexander helped organize the McClintock Presbyterian Church in October 1865. The services were held at Alexander's home, and the white minister not only served as the first pastor, but he also donated land for services. The McClintock School followed later. In 1867, Alexander and Miller helped found the Freedmen's College of North Carolina. A donation of land by former Confederate William Myers was followed by a monetary gift by Mary Biddle, the widow of Union major Henry Biddle, and the school reopened as the Biddle Memorial Institute on Beatties Ford Road in 1868: "an institution in which preachers, teachers and leaders for the colored race might be trained." In 1923, the name of the school was changed to Johnson C. Smith University.[125]

Governor Holden sent out an August 1865 call for the election of delegates in September. The delegates were to attend an October Constitutional convention in Raleigh. Mecklenburg was allowed two delegates. In August, advertisements began to appear in local papers, announcing candidates. One read: "A portion of the loyal citizens of Mecklenburg County nominate Alexander McIver, Esq., of Davidson College (the Chairman of the present County Court), as a candidate to represent Mecklenburg County in the State Convention." McIver won, as did Thomas Alexander. At their October meeting in Raleigh, delegates repealed the secession ordinance and then declared slavery "forever prohibited within the State." They also called for statewide elections the following November, electing positions from governor and congressional representatives to sheriffs.[126]

Running for Congress from the Sixth District were Mecklenburg County native and Union County lawyer Samuel Walkup, former colonel of the Forty-eighth North Carolina Troops; Gaston County's Dr. William Sloan, who proclaimed in an advertisement that his record "will furnish no data for his rejection at the hands of the Federal Congress"; and, Dr. James Ramsay, of Rowan County, a former member of the Confederate Congress as a peace candidate. Running for governor was Holden, with the backing of several North Carolina newspapers, including the *Western Democrat*, and Jonathan Worth, a Quaker and original Unionist from Burlington. Worth was state treasurer for five months in 1865, appointed by Holden in the provisional government. Joseph Wilson of Mecklenburg was running for the state senate, while Robert Whitley and James Hutchison ran for the state house. After the votes were tallied, Worth beat Holden by a majority of 5,939 out of 57,616 votes cast. In Mecklenburg County, 534 votes were cast for Worth, with 353 for Holden. Wilson secured the seat in the state senate, Hutchison and Whitley in the state house. Colonel Walkup won decisively over Ramsay and Sloan for the Congressional seat. The election was a conservative victory, returning many former Confederates to political power across the state. However, the election demonstrated to the radicals in Congress that North Carolina had failed to create new political leadership. "There seems, in many of the elections, something like defiance, which is all out of place at this time," President Johnson wrote. In the end, the Radical members of Congress

Jonathan Worth served as governor of North Carolina from 1865 to 1867. *North Carolina State Archives.*

refused to seat the elected Southern representatives.[127]

There was one other event to play out as 1865 ended. Several newspapermen in North Carolina were arrested for violating an order stating that "until the restoration and full operation of civil laws, publishers of newspapers... will be subject to the restrictions existing under military rule, and will not be permitted to discuss and criticize the acts of the military authorities." The editor of the *Fayetteville News* and the publisher of the *Goldsboro News* were both arrested and tried. The most notable case involved the editor of the *Charlotte Carolina Times*, Robert Waring. The editor wrote in late 1865 that the "South is now under a more grinding despotism that has heretofore found a place on the face of the earth." Waring went on to say that the Russian serf was better off than the defeated South and that Southerners were "the equal, if not the superior, of the mercenary race which now dominates over him." A.W. Chance was working as a pressman for Waring at the time and recalled many years later, of Waring "coming to the composing room, suitcase in hand, with the spirited exclamation: 'Hold the fort, boys: I'll be back again.' With the wave of the hand and his usual pleasant smile, he passed out." The Federal military tried Waring for violating the law. Waring was found guilty and fined three hundred dollars or he would spend six months in prison. It only took him five days to pay the fine.[128]

Charlotte settled to an uneasy peace in 1866. There were still clashes between the Federal officials and former Confederates; many people, however, were busy trying to rebuild their lives. "We are seriously desirous of letting by-gones be bygones," wrote the editor of the *Western Democrat*. "We are tired of turmoil and disputes, and want to do all in our power to promote peace." New businesses and industry were springing up. Yet, North Carolinians struggled to throw off the past.[129]

President Johnson declared the insurrection over on April 2, 1866, in every Southern state save Texas. Unfortunately, this did not relieve the uneasiness felt by the people across North Carolina. Thomas Vail wrote Governor Worth in April 1866, trying to follow up on his request for presidential pardon submitted in December 1865. Worth advised Vail to write "Gov. Holden's agent in Washington…and promise to pay him something if you are willing to do so. I think you can get your pardon quickly." Sheriff John Brown wrote to Governor Worth in August 1866, informing him that John Allen of Mecklenburg had murdered "a negro by the name of Tilus" and that Allen was now a fugitive from justice, possibly in Cabarrus County. In December 1866, the General Assembly passed the Amnesty Act, pardoning civilian and military men for any act of war committed in North Carolina from 1861 to 1865. The act, however, failed to pardon civilians who had served as guides, spies or had failed to enlist when the Confederate government passed the Conscription Act.[130]

In 1867, Congress determined that Presidential Reconstruction had failed, and over the veto of President Johnson, began to implement its own Reconstruction Acts. Congress divided the South into five military districts, with North and South Carolina designated as the Second Military District under the command first of Major General Daniel Sickles, then Brigadier General Edward Canby. For readmittance to the Union, each state had to elect new delegates and draft a new constitution, which would be submitted to Congress for approval. The new constitutions were required to provide the vote to Freedmen, and the new General Assembly elected under the new Constitution was required to ratify the fourteenth amendment to the United States Constitution. In March 1867, the Republican Party was organized in North Carolina by Holden, followed two months later by the Republican Party in Mecklenburg County. The members were a diverse set, including John Schenck, a free mulatto, artisan and Union veteran; farmhand Armstead Brown; black tinner John Davidson; Presbyterian ministers Alexander and Miller; entrepreneur and Confederate veteran William Myers; and former Confederate general Rufus Barringer. They chose Mecklenburg Declaration of Independence Day—May 20,1867—"to declare their liberation from traditional politics." The Colored Union League members formed a line a half-mile long and paraded through town.[131]

Information is scarce about the activities of clandestine organizations. Daniel Tompkins wrote in his *History of Mecklenburg County* that the "Klu-Klux [sic] played no part in Mecklenburg affairs, and though there were a few members in this section, there was not an organization in the county." However, John Alexander wrote that the "only means by which we could combat their devilish meanness was through the Invisible Empire. The Ku Klux Klan was all that saved our country, our women, children and old men." Information on secret liberal or Republican organizations, like the Red Strings or the Colored Union League, is even more scarce.[132]

Elections were called for in October 1867. Out of the 179,653 registered voters, 93,006 voted for the convention, with 32,961 against. The Republicans captured 107 out of the 120 seats for the upcoming constitutional convention. Two Republicans, Edward Fulling and Silas Stillwell, defeated the Conservative candidates to represent Mecklenburg County. At the convention in January 1868, the delegates drew on earlier North Carolina constitutions and those of other states. Abolition and universal male suffrage were included in the new document, along with making representatives, judges and county officials elected positions. Property ownership was no longer required for voting, and the governor's term was increased from two to four years. The elected position of lieutenant governor was added, also serving as the president of the senate. Other changes included a term of eight years for Supreme Court judges, increasing the number of judges from three to five, popular elections of county sheriffs and free public schools for both white and black children. In March 1868, the last Reconstruction act was passed by Congress, calling for a simple majority of votes cast for a state to ratify the new constitution.

The ratification of the new constitution was held alongside a general election. There were 93,084 votes cast for ratification between April 21 and 23, with 74,015 against. Nearly 30,000 registered voters did not cast a vote, some out of political conviction that the whole process was wrong. William Holden was elected governor, and the Republicans carried fifty-eight of eighty-nine counties. On June 25, 1868, North Carolina was readmitted to the Union, and on July 1, Holden was sworn in as governor.

December 1867 brought an end to the continuous occupation of Charlotte by Federal soldiers. Captain Henry Lazella, Eighth United States Infantry, formed his company while Mayor Samuel Harris presented the captain with a resolution adopted by the board of aldermen, thanking the soldiers for their good behavior and expressing regret that the soldiers were leaving the Queen City.[133]

Reconstruction officially ended in the mid-1870s. Charlotte, however, continued to grow and prosper, much more than any other city in North Carolina and most other cities in the South.

Chapter 9

Remembrance: "This Will Be Our Last Parade"

S carcely had the guns grown cold when the mourning process began. Most of the soldiers' aid societies organized during the war were reorganized into Ladies' Memorial Associations. In Fayetteville, ladies obtained a section in Cross Creek Cemetery and began to reinter Confederate soldiers from the surrounding area. Likewise, Raleigh ladies worked to move Confederate dead from the old hospital site to Oakwood Cemetery when the Federal government chose the old site, near the rock quarry, for a national cemetery and required the relocation of Confederate remains.

The establishment of national cemeteries was dictated by the April 13, 1866, passage of a joint resolution in Congress, requiring suitable burial places for the Union dead; honoring the fallen soldiers was certainly not a practice exclusive to grieving Southerners. There were four National Cemeteries in North Carolina: Raleigh, New Bern, Wilmington and Salisbury. At the latter, the government simply took over the existing cemetery. The forty-five Federal soldiers buried in Charlotte were all reinterred at Salisbury National Cemetery.[134]

Caring for the dead was often a laborious task that began soon after the war. According to Lily Long, Fanny Downing became president of the Memorial Association in Charlotte. Its purpose was "to raise funds to give proper burial and a commemorative monument to those that had been laid to rest near us." The group sponsored "concerts, suppers, tableaux, [and] charades" to raise money as early as 1866. The city gave a piece of ground in Elmwood Cemetery, and members of the Segrave family helped locate

It was common for Confederate veterans and members of the United Daughters of the Confederacy to gather jointly. In this 1924 photograph, they are guests of Southern Manufacturing Club in Charlotte. *Donna and Steve Poteet.*

graves. "This was a work of labor and difficulty," Long continued. "The field used for burial was overgrown with briars, weeds and bushes. Most of the head boards had been destroyed...The work proceeded slowly. The graves had to be probed for, and distinguishing marks sought, a shred of grey uniform, a button, or some such slight token often the only certain mark." The majority of the work took place in January and February 1870. By March "169 bodies had been removed to the cemetery, the graves sodden, the plot dressed." A call was issued through the newspaper for "the ladies of Charlotte...to bring flowers and evergreens...at 5½ p.m...to ornament the soldiers' graves" both at Elmwood and at the Old Settlers Cemetery. "A large number obeyed this informal call. No ceremony was observed, but one after another bent forward and laid flowers on the graves, leaving them fragrant mounds of brilliant colors." Thus began Confederate Memorial Day in Charlotte, still recognized as an official state holiday today.[135]

An article appeared a week later, revealing that the group had not raised adequate funds and sought donations to complete the cemetery project. Donations were taken at the First National Bank, the banking house of Tate and Dewey, or at the mayor's office. It is unclear when the last soldier was reinterred at the Confederate section.[136]

The Memorial Association also sought to erect a suitable monument. A marble shaft was dedicated on June 30, 1887. The Memorial Association

raised the funds, and John Wilkes provided the labor. On dedication day, the grounds of Elmwood Cemetery were packed. Reverend E.A. Osborne offered the invocation, and Ham Jones read verses composed by Mrs. B.L. Dewey, an ode "whose pathos drew tears from the audience." Former governor and Charlotte resident Zebulon Baird Vance was the keynote speaker, and the monument was given to the veterans. Not everyone approved of the work of the Ladies Memorial Association. "A widow of a Confederate soldier," reported the *Western Democrat*, thought "it would be better to collect money for relieving the poor widows and orphans…instead of asking donations to aid in the erecting of monuments over the graves of the dead heroes."[137]

A year after the monument's dedication, former Confederate soldiers met at the courthouse on May 10 and organized the Confederate Survivors Association of Mecklenburg County. Captain John Erwin was elected president, while Robert Cochrane was elected secretary. Each township in the county had a vice-president. There were 550 members. A relief committee was "appointed to minister to the wants of any old Confederate soldiers in destitute circumstances," and a cornet band was organized to provide music. The veterans agreed to meet again the second Saturday in August 1888.[138]

In October 1881, at the state fairgrounds in Raleigh, some five hundred veterans created the Society of Ex-Confederate Soldiers and Sailors of North Carolina. In 1889, members of different veterans groups met in

Louisiana and formed the United Confederate Veterans, with former Confederate General John Gordon, commander. The "object and purpose of this organization will be strictly social, literary, historical and benevolent…to gather authentic data for an impartial history of the war… to preserve the relics or mementoes… [and] to care for the disabled and extend a hand to the needy." The Confederate Survivors Association of Mecklenburg County voted to join the national organization in 1893, becoming the Mecklenburg County Camp 382. Rufus Barringer was elected commander of the camp; Harrison Watts, lieutenant commander; D.G. Maxwell, adjutant and secretary; E.A. Osborne, chaplain; and, William Ross, color sergeant. North Carolina had, by 1901, seventy United Confederate Veteran Camps spread out across the state. Many camps met once a year, usually around May 10, Confederate Memorial Day. The Mecklenburg Camp, at least in the late 1890s, 1900s and 1910s, met monthly, first in the Wilkerson Building, and later, in city hall. According to the *Charlotte Observer*, the veterans lined the meeting hall with relics and photographs of local soldiers, politicians and generals.[139]

Each January, the veterans often gathered to celebrate the birthdays of Confederate generals Robert E. Lee and Thomas "Stonewall" Jackson. At times, local schools were closed and guests spoke. According to the *Charlotte Observer*, the observance in 1917 was "the best ever." Dr. Daniel Hill Jr. gave the address at a packed Trinity Methodist Church, followed by dinner at the YMCA. Lee-Jackson Day is still celebrated in some locations across North Carolina.[140]

Each spring, a bazaar was held to raise funds for the support of disabled Confederate veterans. In April 1901, it was held at city hall with booths featuring a tobacconist, art, a country store, fancy needle work and a Dixie booth, with photographs of Jackson and Lee, Confederate flags and currency. Mary Anna Jackson, the "gentle queen of Confederate hearts," was stationed here. Jackson's sword was prominently displayed, along with a coat made from an army blanket belonging to David Oates. Lemonade and candy were available. Similar bazaars continued for at least a decade, with the local chapter of the United Daughters of the Confederacy as principal organizers.[141]

The members of several ladies' memorial organizations met in Tennessee in 1894, creating the United Daughters of the Confederacy, with local groups called chapters. On March 22, 1898, several ladies met at the home of Mary Anna Jackson and organized the Stonewall Jackson Chapter No. 220. The widow of Stonewall was elected president, while the widow of Rufus Barringer,

Margaret Barringer, was vice-president. Julia Alexander, who served as president at least twice, penned a brief history of the chapter, outlining highlights of its work. "To hundreds of veterans of [the] Mecklenburg Camp," wrote Alexander, "monthly luncheons were served; Christmas dinners and gifts given; Veterans Hall furnished; care-taker's salary paid; uniforms purchased; birthday gifts presented; Crosses of Honors bestowed; state reunions entertained; financial aid to the needy; flag and wreath of laurel on each casket of [the] deceased, and marker placed at each grave."[142]

Mary Anna Morrison grew up in Mecklenburg and Lincoln Counties. She married Thomas "Stonewall" Jackson in 1857 and resided in Charlotte for a number of years after his death. *Public Library of Charlotte-Mecklenburg County.*

On two different occasions prior to 1940, the Stonewall Jackson Chapter hosted the state conventions: 1901 and 1915. The 1901 convention was held at the Presbyterian College in October. "[L]ong before the convention met the room was thronged with women who are well known in all North Carolina and whose families have borne noble part in making the best history of the State," reported the newspaper. The 1915 state convention met in the Masonic Hall, with over two hundred delegates. In both instances, the halls were adorned with Confederate flags, "the banners of the 'Lost Cause'" and portraits of former military and political leaders. Music, both orchestral and solos, was offered frequently, entertaining guests.[143]

The Stonewall Chapter also marked war sites in Mecklenburg County. In August 1904, the Stonewall Chapter spearheaded the effort to raise funds and install an iron fence around the Confederate section at Elmwood Cemetery. On June 3, 1910, a iron marker was placed on the Southern Air Line freight depot on East Trade Street, marking the location of the Confederate Naval Yard. "This table," according to the *Charlotte Observer,*

Often, various stores in town decorated their storefronts with displays when the reunions took place. *University of North Carolina–Charlotte.*

"was cast and placed by the Mecklenburg Iron Works, Mr. J. Frank Wilkes, manager," under the direction of the Stonewall Chapter. In 1915, during the state meeting, the Stonewall Chapter placed a marker on Trade Street at the site of the last Confederate cabinet meeting. Over two hundred ladies were present. After prayers, speeches and songs, four little girls, including Anna Jackson Preston, Stonewall Jackson's granddaughter, unveiled the monument. The program ended with the crowd singing "Dixie." Crowds again gathered on September 28, 1927, at the old Alexander Graham Junior High School. A boulder, bearing a plaque commemorating the site of the North Carolina Military Institute, was unveiled by the Stonewall Chapter. The marker specifically honored Daniel Hill, commander of the school at the war's start. "No braver Soldier Ever Trod the Path of Duty," the marker read.[144]

A highlight every year was the annual Confederate Memorial Day program at Elmwood Cemetery, held each May 10. Since the dedication of the Confederate monument at Elmwood Cemetery, the program was overseen by the Confederate Survivors Association. In May 1889, the veterans met at the courthouse and then proceeded to the grounds of the First Presbyterian Church, where they formed ranks and marched to Elmwood Cemetery to decorate the graves. "The procession," recorded the *Charlotte News*, "will be headed by the cornet band, following which will come the members of the Survivor's Association, the Hornet's Nest Riflemen [militia], grade school children, and citizens in carriages and on foot." Confederate Memorial Day programs typically followed similar schedules, with a procession from the church to the cemetery, where "the graves of the Confederates were strewn with flowers," often with musical accompaniment. In 1890, the Charlotte Cornet Band led the procession, followed by the veterans, the Hornet's Nest Rifleman, a local militia group, and school children. Two years later, the Naval battalion band led the parade, with a detachment that fired a salute over the graves before the program ended. The naval battalion then returned to the square, to be inspected and drilled, including an exhibit of its Gatling gun. Led by Lieutenant Commander Harrison Watts, and Color-Bearer W.J. Ross, "with the Confederate flag draped, at the head," the 1893 procession formed at the courthouse and proceeded to the cemetery. The first reference to an orator at the cemetery is recorded in 1894 when former Confederate major Clement Dowd spoke.[145]

During the 1890s, another veterans organization joined the Confederate Veterans in their annual procession: the local post of the Grand Army of the Republic [G.A.R.], a Union veterans' organization. Created in April 1866 in Illinois, the Grand Army of the Potomac was founded on the principles of "Fraternity, Charity and Loyalty." There were twenty-two posts in North Carolina and, in 1897, 400 members statewide. Nationally, the G.A.R. was a powerful political organization with 500,000 members. The Charlotte post, organized in 1890, was named the Hartranft Post Number 40 after Major General John Hartranft. Born in Pennsylvania, Hartranft had served with the Army of the Potomac throughout the War, dying in 1889. According to the 1890 Veterans' Census, which survived the fire that destroyed the rest of the 1890 census, there were twenty-four Union veterans living in Mecklenburg County, along with widows of four Federal soldiers. Until 1896, the Hartranft camp met in the Harty building, moving that year to a room over Thomas and Maxwell's store. The year the post was organized, the Confederate veterans invited the former Federal soldiers to participate in local events, from picnics to the annual Confederate Memorial Day programs. In 1894, this request became a "standing invitation." In 1896, the Hartranft Post likewise extended the invitation to the Confederate veterans to participate in its programs. Each year, the Hartranft Post ventured to Salisbury National Cemetery on Federal Memorial Day to decorate the graves of Union soldiers, usually stopping by Elmwood Cemetery to decorate the Federal graves and place flowers or a wreath at the Confederate Monument. In 1897, the post requested a cannon from the War Department to serve as a monument. According to the *Charlotte Observer* in 1898, not just one cannon, but "two large cannon" were lying unmounted on the grounds of the courthouse. The city did not want them, and the newspaper believed they should be sent to the United States Mint property for display. Commanders of the Hartranft Post included F.S. Eldridge and R.W. Smith. While the Hartranft Post continued until at least 1931, membership was always low. By the turn of the twentieth century, the post disappeared from the list of groups involved in the annual Confederate Memorial Day programs.[146]

While she might have attended before, the local newspapers first made mention of Mary Anna Jackson's presence at the Confederate Memorial Day program in 1900. The widow of Stonewall "was given a seat in front of the monument. At her back was a mound of lilies and roses, and around her were grouped a thousand children." The day's speaker was the Reverend Frank Siler of Trinity Methodist Church. After the graves were bestrewn with flowers, three volleys were fired, and, for the first recorded instance at the program in Charlotte, the bugler sounded taps. The following year was the first mention of presenting veterans with Crosses of Honor. The medal, in the shape of a Maltese cross, with a Confederate battle flag surrounded with a laurel wreath, was only awarded through the United Daughters of the Confederacy. A Confederate veteran who had provided honorable service during the war could submit an application for the award. For many years, the crosses were presented to the veterans during the Confederate Memorial Day activities. Mrs. Jackson herself pinned the crosses on the coats of eleven veterans in 1903. Often she was helped by Margaret Barringer. In 1912, Mrs. Jackson was presented a posthumous Cross of Honor for her famed husband.[147]

By the early 1900s, the Stonewall Chapter of the United Daughters of the Confederacy had taken over the planning of the annual Confederate Memorial Day service. Part of the program moved indoors in 1904, to the Presbyterian College auditorium. The 1908 observance drew roughly three thousand people. In 1913, the fiftieth anniversary of the death of General Jackson, the programs moved to the YMCA. Usually businesses closed early to accommodate the 4:00 p.m. start time, but in 1908, they closed entirely, as did the banks and, at noon, the post offices. Local lawyer L.L. Caudle spoke:

We stand today upon the very spot where freedom was first born in America and where the yoke of British despotism was cast off and it was this same spirit which led the Confederate soldiers to do battle from Bethel to Appomattox...Truer men never lived and braver men never died than those who wore the Gray. We are proud of your history and we would not blot out from memory the mason and dixon line because we would not blot out the brightest gems of American history and the grandest example of patriotism of which the world knows.

The oration and pinning of the Cross of Honor moved to First Baptist Church in 1914. A Confederate flag "was draped across the pulpit," and "a profusion of flowers released a fragrance that permeated" the sanctuary. Also represented that year in the program were the mayor, aldermen, executive board, school board and policemen. The special speaker that year was Victor Bryant.[148]

The observance in 1916 drew only thirty Confederate veterans, and programs were scaled back during World War I. In 1917, the old soldiers assembled at Veterans Hall, within the city hall, and were escorted by the Boy Scouts to Elmwood Cemetery. After a brief speech by Reverend Luther Little, flowers were strewn on the graves of Confederates, but also on the graves of soldiers who had died while stationed at Camp Greene. The program ended with the band playing the "Star Spangled Banner" and the soldiers, young and old alike, at attention, watching as "the sun sank gently below the horizon at the last strains of the national Anthem." In 1920, the Charlotte Observer lamented that "but for the closing of the bank doors, as required under State holiday laws, the business world seems to take but little token of the day. Time was when it was a half holiday for the town, when stores closed, school children paraded and the whole town turned out, marching to the cemetery."[149]

Another annual event was the veterans' picnic. In August 1890, the picnic was held on the grounds of the South Graded School. "There were speeches, dinner, etc., and all had a good time," reported the *Charlotte News*, which wrote that there were 308 veterans in line. The 1892 event was moved to Latta Park, with an estimated 800 Confederate and Union veterans attending. After a business meeting, "orders were passed along the line to charge. The Confederates and their Union allies numbered some 800 or perhaps 1,000, but the preparations made to receive them were too solid to be carried. They did their best, returning to charge again and again as of old, but they could not get away with 405 pounds of barbecued beef and mutton, 90 chickens, 40 hams...with no end of bread and vegetables." On the last day of August 1894, the annual picnic was held at Sharon Presbyterian Church. The late summer picnic often included the elections for camp officers. This year, Louis Leon was chosen as commander. The picnic returned to Latta Park in 1895, with Charlotte's own John Alexander speaking to 475 veterans, as well their family and friends. There appears to have been no 1896 reunion, "as the camp has not as yet received an invitation from any source." August 1897 brought two veterans' picnics: Mount Zion Church, with about 50 veterans in attendance; and at Sharon Presbyterian Church, with the Mecklenburg Camp sending a large delegation. After eating a scrumptious meal, "ice cream, cake, and good cigars were served the veterans for dessert." After visiting Providence Church in 1899, the reunion was again held at Sharon Church in 1900. In 1901, the Mecklenburg Camp struggled to find a location, while the reunion for veterans in northern Mecklenburg County was held at Mount Zion. In 1903, the Mecklenburg Camp joined other veterans at Mount Zion. The practice of dual events continued in 1904, with Mount Zion continuing to host a reunion, and the Mecklenburg Camp attending a picnic at Mallard Creek. The crowd at the Mount Zion veterans' picnic on August 3, 1905, was estimated at 5,000, with 150 veterans present. After dinner, some of the veterans gathered and formed a United Confederate Veterans camp. R.J. Stough was elected commander and D.W. Mayes, adjutant. A separate reunion was held about a week later at Hickory Grove, with about 1,000 people present. The veterans in Charlotte attended the Mount Zion reunion again in 1906, with an estimated 7,000 people in attendance, including 200 veterans. The annual reunion at Mount Zion was quickly replacing all the other reunions in Mecklenburg County. The newspaper estimated the crowd at Mount Zion in 1907 at 8,000 people. Before dinner, it was proposed that a Confederate monument be raised at Mount Zion, and $600 was collected by the end of the day.

The Mallard Springs community also held a picnic that month. The veterans were present, and Alexander spoke. After dinner, the veterans "donned their gray uniforms, got out the old Springfield rifles[,] went through a few motions, [and] marched out into an old field, a part being detached as 'Yankee sharpshooters.' While the others advanced the sharpshooters fired and then fell back as the 'Johnny Rebs' advanced." The Confederate monument at Mount Zion in Cornelius was dedicated in August 1910, with Miss Feriba Stowe having the honor of pulling the cord releasing the coverings. Reunions continued for years; the last one recorded at Mount Zion Methodist Church in Cornelius was held on August 4, 1949.[150]

Monthly meetings, memorial day services and picnics were not the only duties for the Mecklenburg Camp of the United Confederate Veterans,

South Tryon Street, ready for the Confederate Veterans' parade. *University of North Carolina-Charlotte.*

which also routinely participated in the annual May 20 celebration of the Mecklenburg Declaration of Independence. In 1909, members, along with veterans from the Grand Army of the Republic, escorted President William Taft from the Selwyn Hotel to the speaker's stand in front of the courthouse for the annual event. A few veterans formed a drill squad in 1910, electing officers and setting dates for target practice. In 1908, the veterans proposed sponsoring a picnic for "old colored women and men who stayed at home during the civil war and took care of the wives and children of the master of the plantations, who were away fighting for the South." Mr. C. Bunyan Sikes organized a choir composed of Confederate veterans that performed at city hall in December 1907, Pritchard Memorial Baptist Church in January 1908, Belmont Park Presbyterian Church in March 1908 and at Westminster Presbyterian Church the next month. On several dates, the veterans attended the movies en masse, including in 1911 when they watched films taken at the national reunion in Little Rock, Arkansas. In 1915, about sixty members of the Mecklenburg Camp attended a viewing of the *Birth of a Nation.*[151]

Another special event occurred in May 1893. The Confederacy's only president, Jefferson Davis, died in 1889. He was originally interred in New Orleans. Three years later, his family consented for the body's removal to Hollywood Cemetery in Richmond, Virginia. In late May 1893, the transportation process began. Services were held in many of the larger cities on the train's route from Louisiana to Richmond. Since the train was scheduled to reach Charlotte at 4:15 a.m., stopping just long enough to switch engines, only an artillery and rifle salute were planned. The *Charlotte Observer* reported that on May 30, 1893, over two thousand citizens gathered at the station and waited: the train was two hours late. The Hornet's Nest Riflemen and the Queen City Guards fired three volleys each, while the Confederate veterans lined the tracks with a "battle flag furled and draped in crepe." Flowers were taken from the funeral car and sent to Mrs. Jackson, while two bouquets of flowers from Charlotte were added to the arrangements already embellishing the train. Miss Winnie Davis, the president's daughter, was on board, but "did not appear as the train passed here, owing to the earliness of the hour." The other coaches of the special train held the governors of Louisiana, Alabama and Georgia. Soon, the train was on its way. "Charlotte had paid her last tribute—one of flowers and tears."[152]

Confederate veterans were also publically active, though not to the degree of the Grand Army of the Republic. Pensions for Confederate veterans were often a subject of debate. While the United States offered pensions to Union veterans, each Southern state cared for its own veterans, starting just a couple of years after the war. In January 1866, the process began to supply prosthetic legs to disabled veterans. A year later, arms were added to the resolution from the General Assembly. A former soldier who did not need or want the prosthesis could accept cash instead. Three Charlotte veterans applied on May 30, 1866. John Howie of the Fifty-third North Carolina Troops was wounded in the ankle and captured near Winchester, Virginia, on September 5, 1864. A Union doctor amputated his right leg the next day. J.H. McGinn claimed to have served in the Thirteenth North Carolina State Troops, although the records are unclear. He had also lost a leg. Levi Walker, who also served in the Fifty-third North Carolina, was wounded and captured at Gettysburg, losing his left leg to amputation. Overall, seventy residents of Mecklenburg County applied for artificial limbs, an even number each for arms and legs.[153]

In 1885, North Carolina began granting pensions to the disabled and indigent veterans and destitute widows. By 1900, there were seventy-one pensioners in Mecklenburg County, plus forty-one widows. In Charlotte, there were twenty-six men and thirteen women. There was a new pension act in 1901, opening the way for any Confederate veterans who could document their service, and their widows, to receive assistance from the state. The pensioners were divided up into four classes: totally disabled; those who had lost a leg above the knee or arm above the elbow; those who had lost a foot or leg below the knee, or an arm below the elbow or had received a wound that made a limb useless; and those who had lost an eye, were unfit for general labor, or widows. In 1901, first-class pensioners received $72 per year, while fourth-class received $30. By 1903, the number of pensioners in Mecklenburg County had grown to 230, plus 60 widows. There were 2 first class pensioners, 14 second class, 23 third class and 191 fourth class. The 1901 Pension Act was modified several times, including once in 1927 when black men who had served in the Confederate army as cooks and wagoneers became eligible. All counties in North Carolina had pension boards to interview the applicants and facilitate the distribution of funds. In 1893, the pension board was composed of Chairman Thomas Grier, J.H. McClintock, R.A. Torrance, W.B. Taylor and L.J. Walker. Pension checks always arrived annually, at the end of December.[154]

North Carolina took other steps to help Confederate veterans. In 1890, the state opened an old soldiers' home in Raleigh. Each county was responsible for paying the upkeep of the old soldiers lodged there. According to the *Charlotte News*, the first resident admitted at the home was James Sheffield, the tobacconist who served on the C.S.S. *Virginia*. Sheffield died in 1895 and is buried in Oakwood Cemetery in Raleigh.[155]

On different occasions, Charlotte hosted statewide Confederate veteran reunions. The first grand reunion of North Carolina Confederate veterans was held in Charlotte in 1898. The reunion, held during the annual Mecklenburg Declaration of Independence celebration on May 20, brought at least 1,100 veterans to the city, including three black Confederates from Cabarrus County: "A.J. Reed…who fought under General Barringer; Caleb Little, who was with Colonel Hendrick, and Caleb Melchor, who was with Mr. Monroe." One of the highlights of the meeting was the creation of a local camp of the Sons of Confederate Veterans. There had been talk of forming a camp as early as 1895, when the *Charlotte Observer* wrote, "Dr. C.A. Bland is the moving spirit in the affair. He became interested in a similar camp in Charleston, and proposes to get up one in Charlotte." There was a call to organize the camp in December 1896. "It is not the object of this camp to revive sectional feeling," reported the paper, "but to lay with loving hands, flowers on the graves of the Confederate dead and to rescue from oblivion the names of unknown heroes." In February 1897, "everything [was] in readiness to perfect the organization." On February 11, the Stonewall Jackson Camp of the Sons of Confederate Veterans announced its organization. Bland was the commander, and W.K. Yates, adjutant. "Let every one interested in preserving the records of North Carolina's gallant soldiery do all they can to promote the success of Camp Stonewall Jackson," announced the *Observer.* In 1898, the organization spearheaded the effort to repair the Confederate monument at Elmwood Cemetery. The monument originally sat upon a mound, and the Sons ordered granite blocks and had the monument repaired. On May 10, 1898, the Confederate veterans turned over the Elmwood monument to the Sons of Confederate Veterans.[156]

Veterans from across the state gathered in Charlotte on August 25 and 26 for the annual reunion of the North Carolina Division, United Confederate Veterans. The slate was full of distinguished guests. Speakers included Charlotte mayor Thomas Hawkins; E.A. Osborne of the Mecklenburg Camp; state United Confederate Veterans Commander Julian Carr; former governor Thomas Jarvas; and North Carolina Chief Justice Walter Clark. Among the many special events was a reunion of the survivors of the Bethel Regiment, spearheaded by Louis Leon. Overall, an estimated two thousand veterans attended the reunion. On the second day, just over one thousand of the veterans fell into line and with the "roll of drums, in the wake of tattered banners eloquent of martial conflict," marched through the streets of Charlotte. "This will be our last parade," one old veteran said. Yet they continued to march.[157]

Veterans attended reunions farther afield as well. Forty Charlotte veterans boarded a train on May 17, 1903, headed to New Orleans to participate in the National Reunion of the United Confederate Veterans. The Mecklenburg Camp often met a month before the reunions, electing delegates to represent the camp at these national gatherings. About a dozen veterans attended the reunion in Birmingham, Alabama, in June 1908. Forty to fifty veterans traveled to Macon, Georgia, in May 1912. The following year, delegates from the Mecklenburg camp attended the reunion in Gettysburg, Pennsylvania.[158]

For many years, the veterans clamored for Charlotte to host the national reunion of the United Confederate Veterans. While other states hosted repeatedly, this momentous event was held only once in North Carolina. The program began the evening of June 3, 1929, at the Armory Auditorium. This was billed in the program, a sixty-six-page book with history and photographs, as "Pre-Reunion Ceremonies" on the 121st anniversary of Jefferson Davis's birth. Music, speeches and more music were included. Of special note was the introduction of Miss Robina Webb, the great-granddaughter of Jefferson Davis, who had come all the way from Colorado. Wednesday, June 5, brought a luncheon in the ballroom at the Hotel Charlotte, followed by an evening of historical programs. The veterans themselves were meeting at the Armory.

Colton Lynes, commander of the United Confederate Veterans, with various members of the United Daughters of the Confederacy, at the 1929 National Reunion in Charlotte. *University of North Carolina-Charlotte.*

After the call to order on June 5, Judge F. Marion Redd welcomed veterans on behalf of North Carolina. Then came music and welcome speeches by Charlotte mayor George Wilson and Tar Heel governor O. Max Gardner, the president of the Confederate Southern Memorial Association, the president of the United Daughters of the Confederacy and the Commander-in-Chief of the Sons of Confederate Veterans. That was merely the morning session. The afternoon was devoted to different committee reports. That evening, veterans and other attendees could either view the "Grand Historical Drama," entitled "The Rise and Fall of the Confederacy," at the Armory Auditorium, or a concert and address by Charles Brough, wartime governor of Arkansas, at city hall. More business followed on Thursday, June 6. The highlight of the reunion began early on Friday, June 7. Veterans were asked to assemble on the grounds of Camp Goodwyn by 8:00 a.m. "Passing through solid walls of humanity, perhaps the largest crowd ever assembled on the streets of Charlotte, the Confederate parade, climax of the thirty-ninth annual reunion of Confederate veterans, moved to the sound of enthusiastic cheers and wild applause…a line of march said to cover five miles, taking some two hours in passing a given point," reported a veterans' magazine. The *Charlotte Observer* noted that the old veterans

> *did not feel the weight of the years nor the heat of the day; all hearts were in the wave of emotion that swept over them and connected the memories of the past with the glorious results of the day. The parade was more than a line of march; it was a pageant of the South, containing visible expressions of the best that the country has to offer. The bravest of the manhood of the South and the fairest of Southern womanhood were there, glamorous with the emotion that can come only from a deep feeling of patriotism and love.*

An estimated 6,000 people attended the reunion, including at least 3,500 registered veterans. The granddaughter of Stonewall Jackson, Julie Preston, lived in Charlotte with her family and kept an open house, displaying family mementos passed down through the years. A "constant stream of visitors kept her house indeed wide open, and many lingered for a little chat with the gracious hostess."[159]

If anything could be found to mar the reunion, it was the death of two veterans. Cortez Kitchen, commander of the Missouri Division, and John Hancock of Texas, both "crossed over the river" during the reunion. As the attendees were preparing to leave, the Sons of Confederate Veterans dedicated a memorial marker at the new auditorium, commemorating the thirty-ninth annual reunion. The cloth over the marker was drawn by Thomas Jonathan Jackson Preston, the general's great-grandson, and Nancy Palmer Stitt, the granddaughter of Captain William Stitt. Dr. Oren Moore gave the dedication address "and the exercises were closed with taps." The old veterans were soon boarding trains to return to their homes across the nation.[160]

The veterans in Charlotte and Mecklenburg County were crossing over the river themselves. The newspapers were full of the obituaries, and often, members of the Mecklenburg Camp were called on to participate in the funerals, even going as far as to adopt their own ritual for the dead in September 1903. The ritual called for the veterans to gather before the service, wearing a badge of mourning over their left breasts, to escort the dead to the cemetery and, after the body had been lowered into the grave, form a circle. The officer in charge said a few words, ending with, "Rest, soldier, rest. Impartial history will vindicate thy motive and write thy deeds illustrious. Comrade and friend, we give thy body to the dust, and commend thy spirit to God who gave it."[161]

There were no other veterans left in Charlotte to recite these simple words when George W. Benson died on June 14, 1948. Benson was born in Bladen County and served as a private in Company H, Second North Carolina Artillery. He was captured at the fall of Fort Fisher in January 1865, spending the last few months of the war in the prison camp at Point Lookout. He moved to Charlotte after the war. According to his tombstone at Newell Presbyterian Church, Benson was the last survivor of the battle of Fort Fisher. Before long, all of the veterans were gone. The last North Carolina Confederate veteran, Samuel Bennett, died in 1951. With the passing of this gallant band, the Civil War in North Carolina became just a memory.

At Elmwood Cemetery, the Confederate Memorial Day service, usually under the auspices of the Major Egbert Ross Camp of the Sons of Confederate Veterans, still occurs every spring. The event in 1938 was highlighted by the dedication of a memorial arch and plaque, marking the birthplace of Mary Anna Jackson. The widow of Stonewall Jackson died in Charlotte on March 24, 1915. The following day, her body was taken to the First Presbyterian Church, passing through the ranks of old Confederate soldiers. The church was bedecked with wreaths, flowers and Confederate flags. Her casket was borne through the streets to the railroad depot, traveled to Lexington, Virginia, and was interred beside the famous general. Former President Taft sent a letter of condolence, saying that he was "sorry to hear of her passing" and "how proud the people of Charlotte were at having her a fellow citizen." At 11:00 a.m. on Friday, March 26, the hour appointed for the service in Lexington, people gathered all across the South in churches to hold their own memorial services for the beloved widow. The Stonewall Chapter, the Mecklenburg Camp of the United Confederate Veterans and others gathered again at the First Presbyterian Church. Public schools in Charlotte also held their own memorial services. At some point in the 1950s or 1960s, the arch was torn down.[162]

Other monuments and memorials were installed around Charlotte: a marker at the old site of the United States Mint; one to mark the site where Jefferson Davis stood when he heard of the assassination of Abraham Lincoln; a marker designating the Confederate attorney general George Davis's residence during Charlotte's brief stint as the last capital of the Confederacy; and a plaque marking where Confederate secretary of state Judah Benjamin stayed. In 1977, the Confederate Memorial Association of

Charlotte erected a monument beside the old city hall memorializing local Confederate soldiers. In 2000, markers to some of the Mecklenburg County Confederate companies were erected at Elmwood Cemetery.

The work of remembering the war in Charlotte continues to this day.

Afterword

Looking for Civil War Charlotte Today

Standing on the fields of Gettysburg in Pennsylvania or along the banks of Charleston Harbor in South Carolina, one can easily visualize the tragic events of the American Civil War. Countless historical markers and sites tell visitors about the events of 150 years ago. Among the towering skyscrapers in downtown Charlotte, the past does not so obviously beckon. Spires of glass and steel punctuate the skyline of the second-largest banking center in the United States, replacing earlier vestiges of the industrial revolution. Those who seek to find Charlotte's Civil War past today must look carefully.

Probably the best place to begin a tour of Civil War sites is the Charlotte Museum of History, on 3500 Shamrock Drive. The museum also owns and opens for tours the Hezekiah Alexander Homesite. Constructed of native stone in 1774, the Alexander home has witnessed much history as the oldest existing residence in Charlotte. Another informative residence is just three miles away: Historic Rosedale, constructed circa 1815, and today, the site of frequent living histories.

Elmwood Cemetery, on West Sixth Street, is quite possibly the most visible piece of Civil War Charlotte today. Like most cemeteries designed on Victorian principles, Elmwood is an enjoyable public space. Confederates at rest here include Brigadier General Rufus Barringer, the famed cavalry commander and brother-in-law to Stonewall Jackson, and Colonel Charles Lee of the Thirty-seventh North Carolina Troops whose July 1862 funeral closed down the city. Near these two graves is the Confederate section where

Erected in 1887, the Confederate Monument in Elmwood Cemetery marks the graves of over one hundred Confederate soldiers who died in Charlotte during the war. *Author's Collection.*

the monument erected by the Ladies Memorial Association in 1887 still stands guard over the fallen soldiers.

On West Fifth Street, between Poplar and Church Streets, is the Old Settlers' Cemetery. The oldest burial in this cemetery dates from 1776, and other graves include those of numerous early Charlotte leaders and signers of the Mecklenburg Declaration of Independence; several Civil War soldiers are also buried here, including Lieutenant Benjamin Davidson, who died of wounds from the battle of Antietam in August 1862, and Lieutenant James Owens, who served in the Fifty-third North Carolina Troops and was killed in April 1865. Also at rest here is Colonel William Owens, the Charlotte lawyer who was mayor of the Queen City and who lost his life after being wounded at Snicker's Gap, Virginia, on July 19, 1864.

While none of the new North Carolina Civil War Trail markers yet grace the Queen City, there are several older historical markers throughout town. On Trade Street, near Tryon, is the marker denoting the location where the last meeting of the Confederate cabinet occurred on April 26, 1865. On West Trade Street is the historical marker for the old United States Mint. The initial gold rush in the United States had occurred in the area in the

1830s and 1840s; the first United States Mint was established in Charlotte in 1835. The mint building was moved in 1933 and reopened as an art museum that includes displays on its former use, but not on its short stint as the treasury building for the doomed Confederacy.

Markers to famous residents and visitors can still be found, as well. The arch raised to honor Charlotte's beloved Mary Anna Morrison is long gone, but a small plaque remains to testify to its presence. Still standing on North Tryon Street on the grounds of the Old City Hall in bustling downtown is the monument to local Confederate soldiers, which was erected by the Confederate Memorial Association of Charlotte in 1977. Just down the busy thoroughfare, on South Tryon, is the marker embedded in the sidewalk marking the spot where Jefferson Davis was standing when he heard of the death of Abraham Lincoln. On April 19, 1865, Davis was at the Bates home on East Trade Street when he learned Lincoln had been assassinated. Secretary of the navy Stephen Mallory recalled Davis lamenting that "there are a great many men of whose end I would much rather have heard than his. I fear it will be disastrous for our people, and I regret it deeply."

The YMCA on East Morehead Street now sits on the former site of the North Carolina Military Institute. Once the cadets and their professors marched away to the fight, the buildings were used as a medical laboratory, homes for Confederate officials and even as a hospital late in the war. Federal soldiers were garrisoned here during Reconstruction. All the buildings have since tumbled to rubble, but a state historical highway marker remains to mark the location.

Though material vestiges of the war in today's Charlotte are often elusive, the impact of war, Reconstruction and remembrance is a crucial part of the city's history. Those years of struggle, hardship and rebirth helped shape Charlotte as surely as its economic or cultural forces, and an awareness of its unique experiences during the war allows a richer understanding of the Queen City's past, present and future.

Notes

CO	*Charlotte Observer*
CDB	Charlotte Daily Bulletin
CN	Charlotte News
NARA	National Archives and Records Administration
NCW	North Carolina Whig
ORAs	The War of the Rebellion: A Compilation of the Official Records of the Union and Confederate Armies, 128 Vols. Washington, D.C., 1880-1901.
ORNs	Official Records of the Union and Confederate Navies in the War of the Rebellion, 30 Vols. Washington, D.C., 1894-1922.
PLCMC	Public Library of Charlotte and Mecklenburg County
WD	Western Democrat

INTRODUCTION

1. James Walmsley, "The Last Meeting of the Confederate Cabinet," *Mississippi Valley Historical Review* 6 (Dec. 1919), 336, 349.

CHAPTER 1

2. William S. Powell, *North Carolina Through Four Centuries* (Chapel Hill: University of North Carolina Press, 1989), 176.

3. Daniel Tompkins, *History of Mecklenburg County and the City of Charlotte*, 2 vols (Charlotte: Charlotte Chamber of Commerce, 1926), 1:130.

4. Janette Greenwood, *Bittersweet Legacy: The Black and White "Better Classes" in Charlotte, 1850–1910* (Chapel Hill: University of North Carolina Press, 2001), 13–15.

5. Ibid.

6. *WD*, 13 Nov. 1860.

CHAPTER 2

7. *CDB*, 27 Nov. 1860, 1 Dec. 1860.

8. *WD*, 4 Dec. 1860; *Confederate Veteran* 25 (September 1917): 413.

9. *WD*, 4 Dec. 1860.

10. Ibid., 18 Dec. 1860, 1 Jan. 1861, 5 Feb. 1861.

11. Ibid., 26 Feb. 1861, 5 Mar. 1861.

12. Ibid., 19 Mar. 1861, 30 Apr. 1861.

13. Ibid., 16 Apr. 1861.

14. *Confederate Veteran* 23 (Sept. 1915): 400; Walter Clark, *Histories of the Several Regiments and Battalions from North Carolina in the Great War, 1861–1865*, 5 vols. (Raleigh: E.M. Uzzell, 1901), 5:644.

15. Louis Leon, *Diary of a Tar Heel Soldier* (Charlotte: Stone Publishing Company, 1913), 1; ORAs, 1:488.

16. Case Files for Applications from Former Confederates for Presidential Pardons, Record Group 94, Roll 37, NARA.

17. Joseph Sitterson, *The Secession Movement in North Carolina* (Chapel Hill: University of North Carolina Press, 1939), 245.

18. *CDB*, 29 Jan. 1861; Greg Mast, *State Troops and Volunteers* (Raleigh: North Carolina Division of Archives and History, 1995), 78; Louis Manarin et al., *North Carolina Troops*, 18 vols. (Raleigh: North Carolina Division of Archives and History, 1961–present), 5:298.

19. *WD*, 28 May 1861; J.F. Hoke to J.B. Robinson, 27 Apr. 1861, Adjutant Generals Letterbook, North Carolina Department of Archives and History.

20. *WD*, 23 Apr. 1861.

21. *Weekly Raleigh Register*, 15 May 1861.
22. *CO*, 28 Mar. 1917.
23. Clark, *NC Troops*, 1:537; Manarin, *North Carolina Troops*, 1:61–62; 4:270, 442; 5:298; *WD*, 27 Aug. 1861.
24. Wilkes to wife, 4 Aug. 1861, Wilkes Papers, PLCMC; *WD*, 11 Feb. 1862, 4 Jun. 1861; David McAllister, *Genealogical Record of the Descendants of Col. Alexander McAllister* (n.p.: BiblioBazar, 2009), 107.
25. *CDB*, 1 Jul. 1861, 27 Sept. 1861.
26. Allen Trelease, *The North Carolina Railroad, 1849–1871, and the Modernization of North Carolina* (Chapel Hill: University of North Carolina Press, 1991), 140, 159, 183.
27. *CO*, 28 Mar. 1917; *WD*, 2 Jul. 1861.
28. *CDB*, 17 Jul. 1861; *CO*, 20 May 1896; *Fayetteville Observer*, 25 Jul. 1861.
29. Brenda McKean, *Blood and War at My Doorstep*, 2 vols. (n.p.: Xlibiris Corporation, 2011), 1:61; *CDB*, 5 Sept. 1861; Greenwood, *Bittersweet Legacy*, 14.
30. John Wilkes to wife, 26 July 1861, Wilkes Letters, PLCMC.

CHAPTER 3

31. John Wilkes to wife, 2 Sept. 1861, Wilkes papers, PLCMC.
32. *WD*, 21 Jan. 1862.
33. Jeffrey Girvan, ed, *"Deliver Us from This Cruel War": The Civil War Letters of Lieutenant Joseph Hoyle* (Jefferson: McFarland and Company, 2006), 52.
34. *WD*, 18 Feb. 1862; *CDB*, 19 Feb. 1862.
35. *CDB*, 20 Feb. 1862; Walter Hilderman III, *They Went Into the Fight Cheering: Confederate Conscription in North Carolina* (Boone: Parkway Publishing, 2005), 22.
36. *WD*, 19 Aug. 1862; Hilderman, *Into the Fight Cheering*, 49; Manarin, *North Carolina Troops*, 12:85.
37. John Alexander, *Reminiscences of the Past Sixty Years* (Charlotte, privately printed, 1908), 83–84; John B. Alexander to wife, 14 Mar. 1862. Alexander Letters, UNC–Charlotte.
38. *CDB*, 17 Mar. 1862, 9 May 1862; *WD*, 10 Sept. 1861.
39. *CDB*, 24 Mar. 1862.
40. *WD*, 8 Apr. 1862; *CDB*, 14 Apr. 1862, 28 Apr. 1862; Lucy Anderson, *North Carolina Women of the Confederacy* (Fayetteville: 1926), 92.

41. *CDB*, 22 Mar. 1862, 19 Apr. 1862; *WD*, 1 April 1862.

42. *WD*, 10 Jun. 1862; Frontos Johnston, *Zebulon B. Vance, Letters* (Raleigh: North Carolina Department of Archives and History, 1963), 242; *Fayetteville Observer*, 17 Mar. 1862; 6 Feb. 6, 1862; *Weekly Standard*, 23 July 1862.

43. *CDB*, 9 Aug. 1862.

44. *CO*, 20 May 1896; *CDB*, 7 Jul. 1862, 16 Jul. 1862.

45. *NCW*, 8 Jul. 1862.

46. Compiled Service Records of Confederate General and Staff Officers, and Non-regimental Enlisted Men. R.G. 109. M331. Roll 111. NARA; *CDB*, 17 Jul. 1862.

47. *CDB*, 19 Jul. 1862.

48. Ibid., 3 Jul. 1862, 16 Jul. 1862; Marion Howard. CSR. R.G. 109, M331, roll 0133.

49. *CDB*, 28 Nov. 1862.

50. Ibid., 28 Nov. 1862; *Daily Register* (Raleigh), 28 Sept. 1861; "Mecklenburg County Gunpowder Plant," Civil War file, PLCMC, n.d.

51. *CDB*, 20 Feb. 1862, 30 Jun. 1862, 3 Jul. 1862.

52. Violet Alexander, "The Confederate States Navy Yard at Charlotte, N.C., 1862–1865," *Southern Historical Society Papers* 40 (September 1915): 185, 188; William Still Jr. "Facilities for the Construction of War Vessels in the Confederacy," *The Journal of Southern History* 31 (August 1965), 285–304; Subject File of the Confederate States Navy, Record Group 45, M1091, Roll 33, NARA.

53. *The Heritage of Old Mecklenburg County, North Carolina, 1763–2003* (County Heritage, Inc. 2006), 82, 84.

54. *Confederate Veteran*, 24 (May 1916), 238.

55. *CDB*, 28 Nov. 1862; *WD*, 16 Dec. 1862.

56. *WD*, 11 Nov. 1862; *CDB*, 27 Nov. 1862, 3 Dec. 1861.

CHAPTER 4

57. Compiled Service Records of Confederate General and Staff Officers and Assigned Enlisted Men. R.G. 109, M331. Roll 0111. NARA.

58. Alexander Papers, UNC–Charlotte; *WD*, 6 Jan. 1863, 13 Jan. 1863, 7 Apr. 1863; Kathey Herran, *They Married Confederate Officers* (Davidson: Warren Publishing, 1997), 59; Greenwood, *On the Home Front*, 12.

59. *WD*, 17 Mar. 1863, 16 Jun. 1863.

60. Manarin, *North Carolina Troops*, 12:82; *WD*, 17 Feb. 1863.

61. *WD*, 21 Jul. 1863.

62. Louis Brown, ed., "Correspondence of David Olando McRaven and Amanda Nantz McRaven, 1864–1865," *North Carolina Historical Review* 26 (January 1949): 65.

63. *WD*, 12 May 1863; William Hunter, ed., "The Civil War Diaries of Leonard C. Ferguson," *Pennsylvania History* 14 (July 1947): 196, 214.

64. *WD*, 18 Aug. 1863, 15 Sept. 1863, 29 Sept. 1863; Richard Gatlin to Thomas Brem, 14 Sept. 1863, Home Guard Letter Book, AG 52, NCDAH.

65. *WD*, 1 Sept. 1863.

66. ORNs, 2:547; Ralph Donnelly, "The Charlotte, North Carolina, Navy Yard, C.S.N.," *Civil War History* 5 (1959): 72–79.

67. *WD*, 6 Jun. 1863; Ralph Donnelly, "Confederate Acid Works Forgotten Facility of 1864," *CN*, 16 Jan. 1959; D.H. Hill, *North Carolina in the War Between the States* (Edwards & Broughton Company, 1926), 121.

68. *WD*, 26 May 1863, 9 Aug. 1863; 15 Sept. 1863.

69. Ibid., 27 Oct. 1863, 18 Nov. 1863, 24 Nov. 1863.

CHAPTER 5

70. Trelease, *The North Carolina Railroad*, 186; *WD*, 12 Apr. 1864.

71. *WD*, 26 Apr. 1864.

72. Frederic Denison, *Sabres and Spurs: the First Regiment Rhode Island Cavalry in the Civil War* (First Rhode Island Veteran Assn., 1876), 300; *WD*, 31 May 1864.

73. Elizabeth Williams, *A History of the First Presbyterian Church, 1821–1983* (Charlotte, NC: Heritage Press, 1893), 67–8; *WD*, 10 May 1864, 17 May 1864.

74. Carrie McLean, *First Baptist Church, Charlotte, N.C., 1832–1916* (Charlotte, NC: Washburn Press, 1916), 21–22; LeGette Blythe and Charles Brockman, *The Hornet's Nest* (Charlotte, NC: McNally, 2007), 207; Joseph Cheshire, *The Church in the Confederate States: A History of the Protestant Episcopal Church in the Confederate States* (New York: Longmans, Green and Company, 1912), 93.

75. 1864 Tax-in-Kind form, Patterson Papers, UNC-Charlotte; *WD*, 22 Dec. 1863, 27 Mar. 1864.

76. *CDB*, 18 Jan. 1864; *WD*, 9 Aug. 1864.

77. *CO*, 28 Nov. 1896; *CDB*, 7 May 1863.

78. *CDB*, 5 Mar. 1864; Jeff Toalson, *No Soap, No Pay, Diarrhea, Dysentery & Desertion: A Composite Diary of the Last 16 Months of the Confederacy from 1864 to 1865* (Lincoln: iUniverse, 2006), 107.

79. *WD*, 3 May 1864; Manarin, *North Carolina Troops*, 18:169–75.

80. Manarin, *North Carolina Troops*, 18:431–32

81. *WD*, 13 Sept. 1864, 11 Oct. 1864, 23 Oct. 1864.

82. Greenwood, *On the Home Front*, 13; *CO*, 31 Jan. 1915; *WD*, 6 Jan. 1863, 27 Sept. 1864.

CHAPTER 6

83. *WD*, 10 Jan. 1865; Trelease, *The North Carolina Railroad*, 190.

84. *WD*, 21 Feb. 1865; Edmund Burnett, ed., "Letters of a Confederate Surgeon: Dr. Abner Embry McGarity, 1862–1865, part IV, *Georgia Historical Quarterly* 30 (March 1946): 49; ORAs, 47, pt.2: 472.

85. Alexander, *History of Mecklenburg County*, 140–41; *WD*, 29 Nov. 1864, 21 Feb. 1865, 21 Mar. 1865, 30 Mar. 1865.

86. *Report on the Treatment of Prisoners of War by the Rebel Authorities During the War of the Rebellion.* (Washington: Government Printing Office, 1869), 184, 714; A.O. Abbott, *Prison Life in the South* (New York: Harper and Brothers, Publishers, 1865), 177–79; *Confederate Veteran* 26 (Sept. 1918), 127.

87. ORAs, 47, pt. 2:1208, 1239, 1284, 1298; *WD*, 7 Mar. 1865.

88. *CDB*, 21 Mar. 1865, 30 Mar. 1865, 2 Apr. 1865.

89. *CDB*, 2 Apr. 1865, 11 Apr. 1865; *CO*, 17 Feb. 1893.

90. Varina Davis, *Jefferson Davis: Ex-President of the Confederate States of America* (New York, 1890), 2:575; Burton Harrison, "The Capture of Jefferson Davis," *Century Magazine* (Nov. 1883), 130–31; Michael Ballad, *A Long Shadow: Jefferson Davis and the Final Days of the Confederacy* (University Press of Mississippi, 1986), 25; Blythe and Brockmann, *The Hornet's Nest*, 402.

91. Dallas Invine, "The Fate of Confederate Archives: Executive Office," *American Historical Review* 44 (July 1939): 823–41.

92. William Parker, *Recollections of a Confederate Naval Officer* (Annapolis: Naval Institute press, 1985), 272.

93. Chris Hartley, *Stoneman's Raid, 1865* (Winston-Salem, NC: John F. Blair, 2011), 300.

94. Irvine, "Confederate Archives," 826; James Carson, "Heretofore Unpublished Story of Hiding Specie in Woods near Charlotte," newspaper clipping, n.d., PLCMC; Blythe and Brochman, *The Hornet's Nest*, 172; *CDB*, 26 Mar. 1865; "The Ladies" to Colonel Hoke. 19 Apr 1865; Civil War Files, PLCMC.

95. Hartley, *Stoneman's Raid*, 316–17, 320–23.

96. *Confederate Veteran* 15 (Aug. 1907), 366; Harrison, "The Capture of Jefferson Davis," 136; Blythe and Brockmann, *The Hornet's Nest*, 404; Pamela Bennett and Richard Misselhorn, "Curtis R. Burke's Civil War Journal," *Indiana Magazine of History* 67 (June 1971), 155.

97. *CO*, 20 Apr. 1905.

98. Bennett and Misselhorn, "Curtis R. Burke's Journal," 155; Clement Dowd, *The Life of Zebulon Baird Vance* (Charlotte: Observer Printing and Publishing Company, 1897), 486.

99. Walmsley, "The Last Meeting of the Confederate Cabinet," 336–49; Josiah Gorgas, "Confederate Ordinance Department," *Southern Historical Society Papers* 12 (January–February 1884): 91.

100. *Confederate Veteran* 2 (February 1893), 62.

101. William Patterson papers, UNC–Charlotte.

CHAPTER 7

102. William Powell, ed., *Dictionary of North Carolina Biography*, 6 Volumes (Chapel Hill: University of North Carolina Press, 1979), 1:102.

103. Powell, *Dictionary of North Carolina Biography*, 3:132.

104. Michael C. Hardy, *The Thirty-seventh North Carolina Troops: Tar Heels in the Army of Northern Virginia* (Jefferson, NC: McFarland and Company, 2003), 75.

105. Mast, *State Troops*, 78.

106. Manarin, *North Carolina Troops*, 8:111; Francis Casstevens, *The 28ᵗʰ North Carolina Infantry* (Jefferson, NC: McFarland and Company, 2008), 20.

107. Bruce Allardice, *Confederate Colonels* (Columbia: University of Missouri Press, 2008), 296–97.

108. Mauriel Joslyn, *Captives Immortal: The Story of 600 Confederate Officers and the United States Prison of War Policy* (Shippensburg, PA: White Main Publishing, 1996), 22, 48, 58, 65, 85, 99–100, 142.

Chapter 8

109. Hermann Everts, *A Complete and Comprehensive History of the Ninth Regiment New Jersey Vols. Infantry* (A. S. Holbrook, 1865), 177–78; Carson, "Unpublished Story."

110. Everts, *Ninth Regiment New Jersey*, 177–78.

111. ORAs 47, 3:443; Dallas Irvine, "The Fate of Confederate Archives," *American Historical Review* 44 (July 1939): 823–41; *Dallas Weekly Herald* (TX), 1 Jul. 1865.

112. Everts, *Ninth New Jersey*, 179.

113. ORAs 47, 3:458, 497; Tompkins, *History of Mecklenburg County*, 1:143; *Tri-Weekly Bulletin*, 30 May 1865.

114. Manarin, *North Carolina Troops*, 14:344; ORAs 47, 2:1066.

115. Daniel Hill, Roll 39; Margaret Withers, Roll 43; M.W. Alexander, Roll 37; Elam King, Roll 40; Record Group 94, Case Files of Applications from Former Confederates for Presidential Pardons, NARA.

116. *WD*, 6 Jun. 1865.

117. *CO*, 8 April 1894; *WD*, 3 Jul. 1865.

118. *WD*, 13 Jun. 1865.

119. Ibid., 6 Jul. 1865; *CO*, 30 Aug. 1905.

120. Alexander, *History of Mecklenburg County*, 364.

121. Ibid., 363–64; Alexander, *Reminiscences of the Past Sixty Years*, 14; *WD*, 22 Aug. 1865.

122. Barnett to Whittlesey, 27 June 1865, LR, Asst. Comr., RG 105 (NC), NARA; Alexander, *History of Mecklenburg County*, 170; Ruth Blackwelder, *Old Charlotte and Old Mecklenburg Today* (Mecklenburg Historical Association, 1973), 34.

123. Patterson family papers, UNC–Charlotte; Charles Price, "John C. Barnett, Freedmen's Bureau Agents in North Carolina," *Tar Heel Towns, Ship Builders, Reconstructionists, and Alliancemen* (Greenville, TN: ECU Publications, 1891), 51–74.

124. Alexander, *Reminiscences of the Past Sixty Years*, 11; Price, "John C. Barnett," 60–61, 68–69.

125. Greenwood, *Bittersweet Legacy*, 44; *Biennial Report of the Superintendent of Public Instruction of North Carolina* (Raleigh: Edwards and Broughton, 1900), 501.

126. *WD*, 4 Sept. 1865; 3 Oct. 1865; 10 Oct. 1865; 31 Oct. 1865.

127. Ibid., 31 Oct. 1865; 14 Nov. 1865; Eric Foner, *A Short History of Reconstruction* (New York: Harper Row, 1990), 92.

128. *Richmond Times* (VA), 3 Jan. 1866; *CO*, 20 Mar. 1916; Mark Bradley, *Bluecoats & Tar Heels: Soldiers and Civilians in Reconstruction North Carolina* (Lexington: University of Kentucky Press, 2009), 82–83.

129. Greenwood, *Bittersweet Legacy*, 37.

130. J.G. de Roulhac Hamilton, *Correspondence of Worth*, 2 vols. (Raleigh, NC: Edwards and Broughton, 1909), 1:553; John Brown to Worth, 23 Aug. 1866, Governors Papers, North Carolina Department of Archives and History.

131. Greenwood, *Bittersweet Legacy*, 47–48.

132. Tompkins, *History of Mecklenburg County*, 145; Alexander, *Reminiscences of the Past Sixty Years*, 86.

133. Tompkins, *History of Mecklenburg*, 1:44.

Chapter 9

134. *Roll of Honor: The Names of Soldiers Who Died in Defence of the American Union, Interred in the National Cemeteries*, 10 vols. (Government Printing Office, 1869), 10:151–52.

135. *CO*, 20 May 1896; *WD*, 10 May 1870.

136. *WD*, 17 May 1870.

137. *CO*, 22 Mar. 1870, 5 May 1889, 20 May 1898; Raleigh *News and Observer*, 2 Jul. 1887; *WD* 22 Mar. 1870.

138. *CD*, 11 May 1888.

139. *CN*, 9 Sept. 1893; *CO*, 5 Jun. 1905.

140. *CO*, 20 Jan. 1917.

141. Ibid., 4 Apr. 1901.

142. Edwin MacKethan, *Chapter Histories, North Carolina Division, United Daughters of the Confederacy: 1897–1947* (North Carolina Division, United Daughters of the Confederacy, 1947), 51–54.

143. *CO*, 10 Oct. 1901, 6 Oct. 1905.

144. Ibid., 24 Aug. 1904, 5 Jun. 1910, 7 Oct. 1915; S.L. Smith, *North Carolina's Confederate Monuments and Memorials* (North Carolina Division, United Daughters of the Confederacy, 1941), 60.

145. *CN*, 10 May 1889, 5 May 1890; *CO*, 10 May 1892, 11 May 1893, 10 May 1894.

146. Michael C. Hardy, *North Carolina in the Civil War* (Charleston: The History Press, 2011), 132–33; *CO*, 6 May 1890; 23 Apr. 1896, 23 Feb. 1894, 13 Mar. 1918, 9 May 1889.

147. *CO*, 11 May 1900, 10 May 1901, 12 May 1903, 11 May 1912.

148. Ibid., 11 May 1908, 11 May 1913, 10 May 1914, 11 May 1914.

149. Ibid., 11 May 1916, 11 May 1918, 11 May 1920.

150. *CN*, 7 Aug. 1890; *CO*, 19 Aug. 1892, 31 Aug. 1894, 23 Aug. 1895, 4 Aug. 1896, 6 Aug. 1897, 3 Aug. 1897, 19 Aug. 1897, 9 Aug. 1901, 6 Aug. 1904, 4 Aug. 1905, 11 Aug. 1905, 4 Aug. 1906, 2 Aug. 1907, 28 Aug. 1907.

151. *CO*, 25 Sept. 1908, 22 Dec. 1907, 7 Jan. 1908, 1 Mar. 1908, 9 Apr. 1908, 4 Apr. 1909, 18 Dec. 1910, 16 Nov. 1911, 18 Nov. 1915.

152. Ibid., 31 May 1893.

153. Ansley Wegner, *Phantom Pain: North Carolina's Artificial-Limbs Program for Confederate Veterans* (Raleigh: North Carolina Department of Cultural Resources, 2004), 21, 162; Manarin, *North Carolina Troops*, 13:83, 308.

154. *CO*, 2 Jul. 1893, 4 Jul. 1900.

155. *CN*, 1 Jan. 1891.

156. *CO*, 26 May 1895, 27 Dec, 1896, 10 Feb. 1897, 11 Feb. 1897, 24 Apr. 1898, 10 May 1898, 21 May 1898.

157. Ibid., 8 Aug. 1909, 26 Aug. 1908, 27 Aug. 1908, 24 Aug. 1909.

158. Ibid., 18 May 1903, 9 Jun. 1908, 6 May 1912.

159. *Official Program United Confederate Veterans, at their 39ᵗʰ Reunion, Held at Charlotte, N.C.*, 15, 17, 18; "The Reunion in Charlotte," *Confederate Veteran* 37 (July 1929): 245–50.

160. Ibid.

161. *CO*, 4 Sept. 1903

162. *Confederate Veteran* 23 (May 1915), 226; *CO*, 28 Mar. 1915.

Index

C

Charlotte and South Carolina Railroad
  11, 18, 25, 47, 57, 83
churches 23, 30, 31, 48, 49, 59, 76, 86,
  96, 98, 99, 101, 102, 103, 109
Confederate Naval Yard 36, 37, 44,
  51, 97

D

Davis, Jefferson 17, 20, 29, 33, 61, 63,
  64, 66, 70, 80, 103, 106, 109,
  113
Davis, Jefferson 54

E

Elmwood Cemetery 70, 73, 74, 76, 93,
  95, 97, 98, 99, 101, 106, 109,
  110, 111

F

freedmen 85, 86, 89

G

Gibbon, Robert 51, 59, 75, 84
Grand Army of the Republic 99, 103,
  104

H

Harris, Samuel A. 46, 51, 56, 90
Hill, Daniel H. 16, 23, 40, 46, 69, 70,
  72, 74, 81, 98
Holden, William W. 15, 43, 51, 83, 87,
  89, 90
hospitals 34, 35, 39, 51, 59, 76, 80, 85,
  93, 113

J

Jackson, Mary Anna 96, 100, 104, 109
Johnston, Joseph E. 55, 59, 61, 66, 79
Johnston, William 18, 21, 32, 37, 54,
  64

L

Lee, Charles C. 16, 23, 35, 38, 71, 111
Lincoln, Abraham 12, 16, 17, 18, 64,
  70, 109, 113

M

Myers, William 16, 20, 63, 66, 86, 89

N

North Carolina Military Institute 11, 12, 16, 20, 23, 34, 35, 36, 70, 72, 73, 80, 86, 98, 113
North Carolina Railroad 25

O

Old Settlers Cemetery 94
Owens, William 27, 77, 112

P

Page, Richard 37, 44, 51

R

refugees 38, 39, 46, 49, 55, 57, 61, 85
reunions 97, 102, 103, 105, 106

S

slavery 11, 87
slaves 16, 29, 36, 38, 39, 41, 42, 67, 83, 85

U

United Confederate Veterans 96, 102, 106, 109
United Daughters of the Confederacy 96, 100, 107
United States Mint 11, 20, 44, 63, 75, 80, 83, 100, 109, 112

V

Vance, Zebulon Baird 33, 41, 51, 66, 81, 95

W

Wilkes, John 11, 24, 26, 27, 36, 49, 84, 95

Y

Young, John A. 16, 20, 51, 63

About the Author

N orth Carolina's 2010 Historian of the Year, Michael C. Hardy is the author of numerous books, articles and blog posts about the Tar Heels and the Civil War. The books include *North Carolina in the Civil War* (2011), *North Carolina Remembers Gettysburg* (2011), *The Fifty-eighth North Carolina Troops* (2010), *Remembering North Carolina's Confederates* (2006), *The Battle of Hanover Court House* (2006) and the *Thirty-seventh North Carolina Troops* (2003). This study of Charlotte is his sixteenth book. Michael lives with his family in western North Carolina, not far from the famous Grandfather Mountain. He spends time traveling about the state sharing his love of mid-nineteenth-century military history.

Michael C. Hardy, pictured March 2012 at the James K. Polk Birthplace State Historic Site.

Visit us at
www.historypress.net